The Block: A Brooklyn Story

By

Brian O.

ISBN: 0-7596-4219-2

This book is printed on acid free paper.

1stBooks – rev. 04/25/02

Table of Contents

This book is dedicated to my four late block mothers:

Lillias, Louise, Mrs. Jackson…
And my own mother, Merle E. Smith

* * * *

This book is also dedicated to my late block friends
Paul L. Williams and Neal Ebanks

Chapter One

Introduction

Brian O.

It's the new Millenium. As I look back over the past thirty-five years, there's only one constant in my mind... "The Block."

"The Block," Lefferts Avenue, Brooklyn, N.Y., sandwiched between the neighborhoods of Crown Heights and East Flatbush; a block divided between race, culture, and religion. Sometimes this mixture led to volatility, and other times it led to nothing. But on the whole, we all tried to get along... whenever possible.

By the way, the block consisted of basically two types of people. African/Caribbean Americans, and Hasidic Jews. You see, the neighborhoods of Crown Heights and East Flatbush are a melting pot for both of these cultures; and the practice of one-upsmanship, through political means or otherwise, was and still is very rampant. I'll try to bring this out as we go along.

But for now, let's get back to the block. I ran with a group of guys who had a lot in common with me... most of us came from West Indian Heritage. Believe me, on any given day, you could walk into any one of our homes and hear the dialects of Jamaica, Barbados, Cuba, Panama, Honduras, or Grenada. We had families from the South also, and we were pleased to find out how close their culture was to ours.

This led to a camaraderie amongst the guys that have lasted for about thirty-five years... and in all likelihood will continue.

Let's see now, there's Bob, Bart, Larry, Winston, Pat, Sal, Vinny, and Burt... who's no longer with us. OH! And then there's me... Ryan.

We basically got along because there were no over-inflated egos in this group. There were however, people who felt they needed to be heard.

Let's start with Bob. Bob is a classic example of an extremely talented guy with a penchant for the opposite. This guy excelled in whatever he did, but he did certain things better than others; and would choose what he was more deficient in to brag about.

I'll give you an example. Growing up, Bob was the funniest guy on the block. We always said "why don't you become a comedian." But no, Bob felt football was his calling. To listen to him, the NFL needed him, not vice-versa. He eventually became a comedian, but damn, what a hard head.

Now Bart was a football head. That's all he knew. He was the biggest, and liked to flaunt his size. What made Bart unique was that he spoke his own language. He was "Mr. Slang." He made up so many words and sayings, his name should have been called Webster.

Larry was one of the youngest guys on the block. But oh, was he smart. This was mainly because he would look at the mistakes of the older guys and make a concentrated effort not to repeat them. He also had much older brothers to steer him in the right direction. Winston was a laid back kind of guy. His only problem was committing to things too quickly. You could sell him the Brooklyn Bridge.

Pat was the "tinkerer." You give him anything… and he could fix it. Sal started out okay. But something happened to him when he went into the military. When he got out he was never the same. Vinny was a fun-loving daredevil guy, who never took himself too seriously. Burt was the dare devil of the group. He was very daring and courageous. He loved comic books. Burt had a lot of common sense, and felt he didn't need school. I feel that his daredevil ways, and his need to experiment, cost him his life.

Rounding out the group was Boris, who was very high strung. Don the Music Man, Todd, who was always sick, Orlando… the track star, Skeeter, Pat's little brother, Andy, Bob's little brother and block photographer; and Jasper.

We were a very tight-knit group. Kind of like Fat Albert and the Cosby Kids. Only we never played in a junk yard. Right in the middle of the street, that was our playground. Parking a new car on our block was the mistake of a lifetime. We'd play skelley, run races, or play tag… but the game we really took seriously was football. We would be out there all day and all night, trying to dodge each other and ended up banging each other up against cars, fire hydrants, street signs, and street lamps. We were the real precursor to the XFL.

Out of our group of guys, there were two who made these football games fun… Bart and Orlando. Remember, I told you Bart was a football head. Now picture this in your mind. We lived on a small two-way street, with cars parked on each side. So that alone, limited the space we had to play on. We had about seven guys on a side.

Someone would throw the ball off to Bart, and he'd try to run it back; you know like returning a punt. As far as Bart was concerned, on every run back, he managed to elude thirteen people in this narrow area; the ones blocking for him, and the ones trying to tag him. When he eventually would get tagged, he'd throw a tirade, flinging the football to places unseen.

Orlando thought he was a one-man team. If you ever let him play quarterback, that's it; you might as well sit on the sidewalk and read one of Burt's comics. Orlando would call a play in the huddle for another guy, and end up "tucking" the ball away, and like Bart, try to elude thirteen people. His explanation was always the same: "You took too long to get open."

Guys like myself, Larry, Andy, and Todd would just laugh it off. But others like Bart and Winston, would be furious. Bart, because he wanted to be in on every play, and Winston, because he liked to impress the girls while he was playing. Yea, our football was like a religion. You could talk about out sisters, but don't talk about our game. We'd challenge other blocks and win every game.

Then we'd go to the "Bodega" after the game to fill up on junk food and fruits. Bart always gave the proprietor of the store a sad story to get credit… and it always worked. Since he was the biggest, and ate the most, he would hurry up and finish his food; then "house" other guys' food. He was a real glutton.

After we filled our stomachs, we would go play table games; particularly dominoes, spades, or monopoly. For some reason, Andy the photographer, was the best at dominoes, and for the life of me, I didn't know why. Then it dawned on me. Seeing as though Andy was a photographer, he was always paying attention to details; and paying attention to details is a must when playing dominoes.

When we played Monopoly, I won more than I lost; but for some reason the guys always accused me of stealing from the bank. I never did… OK, maybe one time, but the real thief was Bart. He used to steal the money and set me up. Eventually the guys stopped letting me be the banker. They gave the job to Bob. I guess the guys thought since he was too busy telling jokes, stealing the money would be the farthest thing from his mind; and do you know what? They were right. Bob never stole.

Chapter Two

Off the Block Characters

Brian O.

You could never fully understand the nuances of the block without knowing about the "Off the Block Characters." Now many characters walked through that block, but to me these guys stand out: Bob's cousin Kyle, Kyle's cousin Lonnie, Bow-Legged Will, and his brother Rods, Bart's friend Claude, Raul from Flatbush, Carl from East New York, and Mac.

Actually, Kyle lived on the block for a while. He lived with Bob, his cousin. He was a quiet guy, and a master mechanic… but he was no grease monkey, and he kept Bob stable. His cousin Lonnie was sort of daring and excitable, but no where near as daring as Burt. Now he didn't know this, but most of the fellas thought he looked like Groucho Marx. But all in all, he was an okay guy.

Now we come to Bow-Legged Will and his brother Rods. Will was a very smart guy. Sometimes too smart for his own good. He was in a lot of my classes at school, and he attended the same church that I did. To talk to him over the phone, you would never know he had an obsession… but he did… clothes.

Most of the guys would buy clothes off the rack. We'd either go to Delancey Street in Manhattan, or King's Plaza in Brooklyn. But Will would buy fabric, and have some tailor make his clothes. If he bought clothes that were not tailor-made, then they would be the most expensive in the store. As a matter of fact, now that I think about it, he was the most extravagant guy out of all of us. Why? Only a psychiatrist knows. But all in all, he was my "partner."

His brother Rods, now that's another story. He was the storm to his brother's calm. The Mr. Hyde to Will's Dr. Jeckyl. Do you remember that TV show, The Incredible Hulk? Do you remember that split screen in the beginning of the show that has Dr. Banner on one side, and the Hulk on the other? That's Will and Rods. Rods at one time was one hell of a baseball player. We all thought if anyone was going to play professional baseball, it was going to be him. He always walked around with a glove, and loved the St. Louis Cardinals. He was a Lou Brock "freak."

Then something went wrong. He started lifting weights and taking up karate. He started eating raw everything. Everything he did had to be perfect. Then suddenly, it happened. All of sudden, he "snapped." He hasn't been the same since. Rods became a victim of mental illness. It tugs at him every day. Sometimes he wins, sometimes he loses. But I admire him greatly for his effort.

Claude!! What can I say about him. He was a close friend of Bart. They were like brothers. Like Bart, Claude was a big guy. But he had a more gentle nature than Bart. He also stuttered greatly, which made him the butt of many jokes. But Claude always listened to what you had to say. He had a very sympathetic ear. Because of this, even though he was a big guy, he was less intimidating than Bart. It took a lot to get him mad. But there was a point that you couldn't go beyond. If Claude retaliated against you, you really had to do something to get under his skin. Claude also kept a lot of stuff in. "Unpredictable triggers" could be very dangerous around this guy.

Raul from Flatbush? What can I say. We also attended the same church. Raul was an enigma. On the one hand, he was well read, and very studious. On the other hand, he was very "street." An excellent graffiti artist, and a hell of a D.J. This guy could spin records with his eyes closed. He was that good. He couldn't dance a lick, but hey, you can't have everything. Raul also like fast cars, and alcohol. Sometimes that could be a volatile mix. But he had a handle on things. He was also another guy who could fix almost anything. He and I had a lot of good times. Raul liked being in the company of Bob. Bob's comedic antics would keep him in stitches. Raul was my buddy, though his one main flaw was worrying about what people thought of him.

Now Carl from East New York was a ladies' man. I met Carl at one of my many places of employment. This guy was a smooth character. He had fancy clothes and was a snappy dresser. What made Carl unique was his Guyanese accent. He flaunted it, and the ladies ate it up. He also had fancy cars. You name it, he had it. Carl was a good guy to hang out with, because women would "trickle out of his cup," into your lap… if you catch my drift. And his generosity made it that much easier.

I put Mac in my off-the-block-characters group. But to be quite honest, he lived on the block. The problem is, he moved off the block early. But at times, like a "bolt out of the blue," he would just reappear. Don't ask me where he was coming from. He would just show up. His family was from the South, so I guess he was "hanging out" down there. Mac was a "kool" guy with a funny southern accent.

Of course there were other off-the-block-characters, but these guys stick out in my mind. If I mentioned all of the off-the-block characters, I'd never get out of this chapter; and I have a long way to go.

This bunch of Block Characters and Off-The-Block Characters made for a very interesting mix on "The Block." Each one of these guys had their own unique style, and brought it to the "Block's Table." But I don't want you all to think "The Block" was full of guys. We had stray cats, squirrels, big black junkyard dogs… and oh, yes, the fairer sex. The Girls. And what a bunch of characters they were. Some were quiet, some were loud. But as you'll see in my next chapter, they were the unofficial "pulse" of "The Block."

Chapter Three

The Girls

Brian O.

I bet you thought I would be talking about the fellas throughout this book. Now, what kind of guy would I be if I didn't mention the girls. They were a motley crew, a bunch of characters. Let's see, there was Joan, Lettie, Ronnie, Nydia, Eljay, Olivia, Bernice, Vanny, Vangy, Marie, Detty, Dina, Boris' sisters: Cheyenne, Caroline, Jane, and Jennifer; and Leaf.

Let's start with Joan. She didn't know this, but I called her the "Leader." This is not because she was one of the oldest on the "block," it's because she had a commanding "air" about her; and the other girls would listen. Joan should have gone into the military. She would have been an excellent officer. She also liked dogs. She had one that would drag her along the street as she walked it. Damn, that dog was big. Joan would scare us with that dog too.

Lettie was a match waiting to be lit. She was okay, but could "spit fire" at any time. Joan was the only one who could calm her down. One thing I'll say about Lettie, she was the first to make friends with someone when they moved onto "the block." But man, did that mouth have volume. She also was a great cook. Lettie and Boris' sisters could cook anyone under the table.

Ronnie was the silent type. But you always knew she had a lot on her mind. She was so quiet, that you would never hear her walking down the street. If she didn't say anything during a conversation, you would never know she was there. Like I said, she was always deep in thought. I heard she wound up taking a bad turn on the "substance abuse highway." I liked her though, and if I met her today, I'd give her all the support I could. She was okay. Nydia was a blow hard. Let me explain. Unlike Lettie, who blew up only when she had reason to, Nydia blew up all the time. She had to be heard and seen. She needed the stern, calming influence of Joan often. That's all I'll say about her.

Eljay was okay also. She was in a lot of my classes at school. She was funny. Eljay thought she could sing. What a laugh. I must admit though, later on in life, her singing did get better; but I'd never tell her that. Eljay also had these big eyes. You could see her peepers from two blocks away. She was also very sweet; and she wasn't a loud mouth. Eljay was semi-excitable though. If she liked something she ran with it. I'll give you an example. If Eljay thought "Trix" was better than "Lucky Charms," there was nothing you were going to say to change her mind. That went for music, clothes, guys... anything.

Eljay's sister, Olivia, was a bit more stable. At least I felt so. She was one of the younger girls. Olivia could cook too. But I felt Olivia should have been living in the 1920's... participating in the Women's Suffrage Movement. She always took a stand on something, and could have a real combative streak in her when she wanted to. She was also a computer head; and I've never seen a girl that loved to wear silver as much as her.

Bernice, now there was a looker. Bob really dug her. She was quiet, and always smiling. Bernice was very laid back. I think you could light a match to her feet, and she wouldn't even say 'ow.' As a matter of fact, I never heard her say more than three words at a time. Now Bob was always buzzing around her, so I'm sure he heard more words than me. He would try to sneak a kiss here and there, and then when he got one, he'd be on cloud nine for the rest of the day. I think she was just playing with his head.

Vanny was the carbon-copy of a brainiac. She was very studious. She always had her head in a book. Vanny skipped grades like rocks skimming a pond surface. None of the guys chased her. I guess it's because her glasses were too thick. They should have hired her for that movie "Revenge of the Nerds." However I must say, Vanny was very giving. She would give you her last piece of gum. And sometimes, she'd do your homework.

Now you see the way Bob used to buzz around Bernice? That's how Vangy used to buzz around Bob. She adored Bob, but Bob being the comedian that he was, used to insult her all the time. When the insults didn't work, he used to threaten to beat her up. I mean, c'mon, she didn't look that bad. Her father used to let us play pool in his basement; until Bart broke his pool stick and hid it behind a couch. That was it!! No more pool. But you know what? If Bob would have kissed Vangy on the cheek just once, and showed just a little interest in her, we'd have been back in the basement playing pool. Instead, he treated her like she had the plague.

Marie was the little sister of Orlando. She was a legend in her own mind. Her plans for the future changed as much as the months. One minute she wanted to be a model, another day she wanted to be an actress. One day she wanted to be an author, the next day she wanted to be a teacher. She eventually settled on the latter. Marie was all right, but there was one thing about her that I didn't like. She would make statements and accusations on a whim, without really knowing what she was talking about; and she had a touch of arrogance. Her saving grace however, was that she could take a joke. One day, while at her house hanging out, Bob and myself caught her eating "beans and hash." Bob has called her that ever since… "beans and hash." Now we come to Dettie. She had "fire in the belly." A West Indian hellcat. She was tough, but she was also fair. She was also very protective of her brothers. Dettie hung out with a lot of Rastafarians. Now I hate to equate Rastafarians with marijuana, because I truly believe not all Rastafarians smoke the plant. They are sort of guilty by association. But damn, Dettie sure did; and she didn't try to hide it. She also took no crap from the Hasidim on the block. If one of the Jews "stepped out of line" around her, they would get a plethora of Jamaican "cuss" words spewed at them. Dettie almost always had a weapon on her also; and wasn't afraid to use it. She got shot one year in the leg, and walked to the hospital herself. Now that's tough.

Boris had four sisters: Cheyenne, Caroline, Jane, and Joyce. They were four-of-a-kind. Cheyenne was one hell of a cook... who loved to bake fruitcake. Caroline was the oldest. She was an arbitrator, who could break up any fight on the street. She could cook too, but not like Cheyenne. She would also raise her fists, to protect her brother. Like Dettie, she would fight a man in a minute. Jane was the brainiac of their family. She was a hell of a mathematician. Jane was very quiet. But no one ever crossed her. She only had to say something once, and you listened. Now, I never saw her "break on someone," but I always had the feeling she'd "kick somebody's ass" if she had to. Jane never hung out on the block. Her playground was the local college. Boris' sister Joyce never spoke often. I think she had some kind of inferiority complex. Seems to me like Joyce was afraid to talk. Why, I don't know. We all liked her. It just seemed like something was bothering her deep down inside. Maybe something traumatic happened to her as a child. Whatever it was, Joyce had a strange aura about her.

Dina was Olivia's next-door neighbor; and best friend. If Olivia was Batman, Dina would be Robin. They were very close. Now I wouldn't say Dina was a follower, but at times it did appear that she sought Olivia's approval on certain issues. One thing about Dina though, she was always well-dressed. She had immaculate grooming skills. Dina was another one who didn't talk much. She made it her point to act like a lady. She would have been an excellent Southern Belle in the 19th Century. Sometimes Dina's cousin Lauren lived at her home. Lauren was more of a free spirit. Unlike Dina, Lauren would let her hair down. She was much more easy going… less uptight. The guys loved her rebellious nature. Last, but certainly not least, we have Leaf. Leaf was Vinny's sister. She should have been a news reporter. She had her ears to the ground. Leaf had something on everyone. What she didn't know however, was that we all had something on her. She didn't know it, but for some strange reason, her life was like an open book. Leaf also tried to fit in greatly. She would go with anybody's flow… just to "be down." I liked Leaf though; she had good conversation. I always felt she should have been a journalism major in college. Why she never realized this, I'll never know.

Yea, the girls were the pulse of "The Block." Like it or not, we needed them just as much as they needed us.

Brian O.

Chapter Four

The Hasidim

Brian O.

I couldn't write about "the block," without mentioning the Hasidic Jews. They were leery of us, just as much as we were leery of them. We had more reason to be on our guard. This was simply because, if we made a complaint to the local precinct about them, nine times out of ten, the police wouldn't show up. But if they made a complaint on us, the cops would come in droves.

The culture barrier was astounding. They didn't understand West Indians, and we for damn sure didn't understand them. Some Hasidim got along with us fine. We had no problems with Mendi, Schlimie and "Long John." But on the whole, you could never quite let your guard down when you dealt with them.

They were also more political than we were. What the hell, we lived in New York City. Some parts of the place is "hymie town." I'm not being anti-semitic either. That's just the fact. It always bothered me, that the Hasidic Jews could say just about anything they wanted about anybody. But as soon as you expressed your views about them on anything, you were considered anti-semitic. If you criticized them for double-parking, or hitting your car while they backed out of a driveway, you were anti-semitic. What a "crock of shit."

I must say though, that the "baby boomer" Hasidims' were more progressive. They didn't have the hang-ups that their parents and others from the "old country" had. Hell, some of them even listened to "rap music."

The older Hasidim were much more defensive. But then again, they might have had reason to be. I'll give you an example... I used to take my shoes to get fixed at a Cobbler on Kingston Avenue. Kingston Avenue, between Empire Boulevard and Eastern Parkway was the Mecca of Hasidic business, and the world headquarters of their religion. Well anyway, whenever I walked into this shoemaker's shop, this Cobbler would be extremely hostile and belligerent. I never knew why. He wouldn't get that way toward the Jewish kids, why me? Then one day as he was giving me my shoes, I noticed numbers on his forearm, near his wrist. Curiosity got the best of me, so I asked him where the numbers came from. He yelled at me and told me to leave his store; and never come back. He said take your shoes somewhere else "boy." Now my mother always told me not to talk back to grown people, so I left his store. As I was leaving his shop, there was a young Jewish woman at the door. She heard the commotion. She walked with me out of the shop, and explained to me that the cobbler got those numbers tattooed on him while in a concentration camp called "Treblinka."

She said to me that his generation of Jews were toughened by the holocaust experience; and find it hard to trust people of other religions and races. Now with me being a kid of eleven years old, I didn't fully understand what went on during the Nazi regime, but I did know this: the people that put the Jews in those concentration camps had the same skin color as them. So why were they so arrogant towards us? As a matter of fact, later on I found out, that although the U.S. Army was segregated during World War II, certain Black Regiments were among the first to liberate Jews from concentration camps. The Hasidim tried to adopt an "Overseer Policy" in the neighborhood. They would oftentimes ride around the neighborhood in unmarked cars, claiming to protect their own, and all the while spewing insults and obscenities at us. I remember the time, not too long ago, when some Hasidim attacked a friend of mine. They accidentally mistook him for someone else. Split his head wide open.

They tried to say my friend instigated this incident. But an investigation proved he didn't. I sure hope he has a good lawyer.

Ironically, there were times that we used to call the Hasidim "The Storm Troopers." This was because, on the few occasions that the police did arrest one of them, they would gather up a mob, and storm the precinct. They would jump on police cars and destroy property; and you know what? The cops would never fire one shot (of anything). Now if we did anything like that, someone in the crowd would wind up injured or dead.

When the Hasidim had their celebrations, we never complained that they were too loud; and folks, let me tell you, they were loud. Sometimes, their festivals would last a whole week. We had one day. Labor Day. On that day, we had the West Indian American parade. The parade came right down Eastern Parkway. Part of Eastern Parkway was the center of the Hasidic Culture. Well they didn't like the fact that this parade was so close to their headquarters. They complained year in and year out. Thankfully, the parade continues to this day. But if it was left up to them, it would be "endsville" for that parade.

Hey… I'm straying away from "the block," aren't I. Well I can give you a good example of "Hasidic highjinks" right on Lefferts Avenue. This had to do with a murder. A few years ago, a Jewish woman was killed on the block… right in her house. Reports varied. Originally, the police were looking for someone in their community. I guess they thought that since the Hasidim were such a closely knit group, the women must have known the killer. After all, the woman was murdered in her house. Originally, I heard that police were looking for someone in a white van. It was reported that a white van was seen leaving the woman's house around the time of the murder. To me this has validity, because I had a white van at that time, and when I came down the street and parked it, the police asked me questions… like "where were you two hours ago," etc.

A Hasidic guy who lived on the block rushed to my aid, telling the police that I live on the block. He had to "clear" me, or else who knows what might have happened. The cops interviewed other blacks on the block also. I specifically remember Andy telling them that he too, saw a white van parked in the woman's driveway. I guess Andy didn't have his camera that day. He could have cleared up a lot of controversy. In any event, the police finally picked up some vagrant, and charged him with the crime. They said his fingerprints were in the house. But for all we know, this guy could have entered the house after the murder was committed. After all, the door was left open and anyone could have walked in. It's quite possible that this vagrant could have walked in the house to pilfer, stumbled upon the murder, and left his fingerprints all over the place. That's all you need to be convicted in this neighborhood if you're black. In the meantime, the guys in the van, whom eyewitnesses reported as white… are forgotten about. Go figure.

Now I'm not going to tell you that as children, we didn't bother the Hasidim. We caused mischief on more than one occasion. Let me give you an example. Burt the daring one, had an eight millimeter projector when we were teenagers. On Saturday when it was the Jewish Sabbath, he would aim his projector from his home across the street onto the synagogue wall, showing pornographic movies. Now that wasn't right. C'mon, that's their place of worship.

On another occasion, we'd play "punch ball" in one of our driveways across the street. There would be old Jewish women sitting on their porch "getting sun." We'd punch the ball with the sole purpose of hitting one of them. It was a rubber ball, so it wouldn't hurt them. But you should have seen the look on their faces when a ball landed in their lap. They would complain, and we always told them that we didn't expect the ball to go that far. You see, another incentive was this; if the ball went over the roof across the street, it was an automatic homerun. So we were always aiming there. But we knew good and damn well that more times than not, we'd fail… and the ball would land on the porch where the old ladies were sitting. We hid our mischief behind the "homerun."

Probably, the single most devastating incident in our neighborhood was the Crown Heights riots of 1991. Hey, it helped topple New York City's first black mayor. Why you ask? There's only one thing I can think of, "Hasidic Appeasement." Let's start from the top. A vehicle carrying the head of the Hasidim runs a red light across a major thoroughfare, and hits two black children. One dies, the other is crippled. Original reports said the driver of the car was drunk. Classic case of running a red light, drunken driving, and vehicular manslaughter, right? Wrong. The driver got off scott free. Throw in the fact that his license was suspended, and he was able to flee the country… and what do you have? Favoritism, political style. After this happened, Black people became livid; and I feel, justifiably so. They protested in front of the Hasidim Headquarters; and fights broke out in the streets. Cars were destroyed. A Jewish man got stabbed twice in the melee. He was rushed to the local hospital. Doctors treated one stab wound, but didn't notice the other one; resulting in the man's death.

Immediately, the Hasidim jumped into action. They demanded justice. They said the mayor of this fair city told the cops to "stand down," thus in effect, cause this man's death to happen. Two Black men were arrested. One for the actual stabbing, and one for inciting a riot.

Now you tell me, how could they pinpoint one man out of hundreds, for inciting a riot? Even if they caught him on camera, the camera would have had to start recording as soon as the riot started... to pick up everything.

Eventually, these two Black men were found guilty of this crime. Now I'm not defending these two guys. I don't know their character. All I know is what I read in the papers. But when the Jewish guy died, the Jews got the results they sought. They got sympathy from the media, here and abroad. The deceased was practically hailed as a saint. I have no doubt he was a nice guy. They said he was a scholar, and I admire anyone who studies. But two things still bother me about the "uprising" to this day. Number one, how was the driver allowed to leave the country with no prosecution; and last but certainly not least, why didn't the media... foreign or domestic, cover the plight of the two little black kids as much as they did the Jewish scholar? Why? I'll tell you why. Because the "powers that be" felt the Jew was more important.

Chapter Five

The Gangs

Brian O.

You know street gangs come and go. Now it's the Bloods and the Crypts. Gangs that originated in California. To me and others of my generation, that just sounds plain stupid. In my day, we never followed anyone's lead. Least of all people that lived three thousand miles away.

When we were growing up there were many gangs in New York City. We had the Black Spades in the Bronx, and the 113 Hellcats in a certain part of Brooklyn. But in our neighborhood, there were three that deserve special mention... The Jolly Stompers, The Tomahawks, and the Ex-Cons. These gangs didn't originate in some "surfer state." They came from right here. New York City. Where concrete is king; and the El-Trains make neighborhoods look like something out of the old "Dark Shadows" TV show.

I would have to say, that the gang we had the most interactions with, were the Jolly Stompers. They were formed "around the way," "drafting" guys as soon as they reached adolescence. We knew many of them before they became gang members. They were just regular guys, who played pick-up basketball games with us in neighborhood parks. But when they became gang members, they thought the neighborhood was theirs. The "Stompers" to me were kind of "schizophrenic." One minute they wanted to be neighborhood protectors, the other minute they wanted to terrorize. Their turf spread through Crown Heights, East Flatbush, Flatbush, and part of Brownsville.

Now at the corner of the block, was "Albany Park." Well the official name of the park was called "Hamilton Metz park." But who the hell was he? It was called Albany Park to the neighborhood "homeys" and especially "The Stompers." Albany Park (located on Albany and Lefferts Avenues) was "ground zero" to the Stompers' world. Now they had their main headquarters elsewhere, in an apartment building; but they hung out at Albany.

Our block was the "thoroughfare," the "interstate," the "yellow brick road," to Albany Park. The Stompers paraded through "the block" to reach their "Shangri-la."

The block guys knew most of them, so most of the time they wouldn't bother us. There were times they would challenge us to a football game. We were better players than they were, but because of situations beyond our control, we would let them win... if you know what I mean. When you're playing against guys named "Chopper," "Slugger," "Pumpkin," and "Rasheem," you don't want to get those guys too riled up.

I guess hindsight being what it is, things could have been a lot worse. The Stompers could have picked on us every time they came down "the block." But they didn't. Maybe it's because they knew there was a cop living on the block. Or maybe it's because they knew the Jews had political clout. Or maybe, just maybe, the Stompers had more important issues to deal with in Albany Park. The Tomahawks!! Now they were a more cohesive gang. They were generally from Brownsville... east of Albany Park. The Tomahawks were more of an organization. They could easily have been a "fortune 500 gang." Their park/headquarters was in a park called Lincoln Terrace. I met most of those guys in school. They were the type of guys who would take your lunch money, or throw your sneakers on the telephone line... in the month of January. Now the only time we would encounter Tomahawks (besides school), was when we'd venture to Pitkin Avenue. Pitkin Avenue was a shopping area. You could get almost anything around there... from clothes to fish. Pitkin Avenue was Tomahawk country. When you walked through there, you held onto your dollars tightly; because you would never know when the Tomahawks were around the corner.

The Tomahawks were like the mob. They were money earners. The lower level Tomahawks would "shake people down," and deliver the booty to the gang hierarchy.

I don't recall them coming down "the block" too often. The block was closer to Stomper country. The Tomahawks would venture down "the block" only when they were going to Albany Park to have some kind of "pow-wow" with the Stompers. The Stompers and Tomahawks didn't rumble. They were what you'd call "family." They would team up and fight other gangs. I guess they thought that in unity there would be strength.

The Ex-Cons were the most deadly gang of all. I'll tell you why. This gang had a lot of older guys. To be in this gang, you had to serve a jail sentence. By far, the Ex-Cons were the wealthiest gang. They had vans, and would ride around the neighborhood "firing off" shots; threatening to kill certain members of other gangs.

The Ex-Cons never walked down the block. They rode. We never spoke to them, and they never spoke to us. We never knew what was in those vans. All we knew was that they were much older than us; and deadly.

I don't recall them holding people up either. They were into things like "drug dealing," burglaries, and extortion. Let's face it! They were the "grown-up" gang. And when the Jolly Stompers and Tomahawks stood in their way, they sought retribution. They had no interest in joining "the family." What they wanted was total gang domination. At their peak, the Stompers and Tomahawks went underground. I guess you could say the Stompers and Tomahawks were terrorized. Did they deserve it. I would say so. You know, what goes around comes around. You know what they say… meet a bully head on and they will blink. Hey, the Ex-Cons made the other two blink so much, you thought they had "sand in their eyes."

Then a funny thing happened. As promptly as they appeared on the scene… they vanished. Like a puff of smoke. My guess is that the Ex-Cons violated their parole, and winded up back in prison. But it is the opinion of this writer that they sounded the death knell of the other two.

I can't conclude this chapter without writing about instances of gang violence. I remember a guy named Bennie, shot in his head at a party… because he wouldn't join the Stompers. I remember a guy beaten with a chain, because he refused to join the Tomahawks. One day, a guy got stabbed in his stomach so bad, you could see some of his intestines. And why?… because he was trying to "rap" to a girl who was a girlfriend of a Tomahawk. Very silly shit.

Guys would get beaten up because they stepped on some gang dude's sneaker… by accident.

Yea you always had to look over your shoulder when the gangs were around. I remember the time when Bob, Sal, and I were on our way to the neighborhood skating rink. We were confronted by gang members. They asked us for money. Bob cajoled his way out of trouble. He had comedic talent even back then. Sal, who thought he had "gang backing," acted feisty; and got this money taken. Me, that evening I guess you could say I blended in with the street shadows. While the gang members confronted the other two, I ducked into the street shadows and kept on walking. Call it "divine intervention," but I was spared a gang confrontation that day. Yea these guys were tough, but where would "the block" have been without them.

Strangely enough, they were part of our block's identity.

Brian O.

Chapter Six

Albany Park

Brian O.

Albany Park, "ground zero," the "Mecca of Mayhem." You want it, "the Park" had it. Sports, gangs, girls, music, movies, you name it. This park was the center of attention in our neck of the woods.

Now Brooklyn had bigger parks… such as Prospect and Lincoln Terrace. But those parks weren't as personable as Albany. Albany was a more comfortable park. Everybody knew everybody.

The guys would play basketball, baseball, or handball. They had one eye on the game, and the other eye on the girls. The girls would sit on the benches with their radios, and just "profile."

Everything happened at Albany. They had picnics, tournaments (of all sorts), gang activity, dances, and even movies. Albany Park is the first place many of us saw "To Sir With Love." Before that, I never even knew who Sidney Poitier was. Hell, Albany even had the Boy Scouts.

Some parents from "the block" never wanted us to go to Albany. I guess they were afraid of the gang element. But the activities in the park made us gravitate to it. Plus we went to school with guys who hung out in the park. Also most of the guys from the block were very level-headed. We knew our limits. We also knew that we had strict West Indian parents, who would "beat your ass at the drop of a dime." And unlike today, if another guy's parent caught you doing something you weren't supposed to be doing… you'd get chastised by them. Then they'd tell your parents, and automatically, there's another whipping. I never heard of B.C.W. in those days.

Like I said, on many occasions we gravitated to Albany Park. There was a challenge there. Let me give you an example. We played basketball on our block amongst the guys. But we never knew how good we were until we took our game to Albany. They

had guys from all over the neighborhood. So your game was really tested.

Guys like Bob, Bart, and Sal, who were really good basketball players, found themselves at Albany a lot. They craved the competition.

Don, Raul and I went to the park for the music. They had excellent D.J.'s at the park, and we three loved that kind of stuff. We would always challenge each other to see who could "spin the best mixes." When we went to the park we would hear "mixes," and then go home and try to copy it. Raul was usually the best, followed by Don… but hey, I held my own. I was the "honorable mention" type.

The park also had a potentially romantic combination… nighttime movies and the ladies.

In the summertime, Albany Park would show classic movies. I guess the "powers that be" felt it was a way to keep things civilized. Now these movies would be shown in the nighttime, and the guys and gals would come out in their best.

Girls and guys would pair off and watch the movies together. Liquor and "weed" (marijuana) would be smuggled in. Throw in the munchies (junk food), and movie night was something special. Besides, movie night might have been one of the few times the gangs didn't' bother you. They were too busy trying to get their "groove on" with the ladies.

Up on the screen, we saw classic movies like "To Sir, With Love," "Bridge Over the River Kwai," "West Side Story," and "The Learning Tree." I guess the gangs really got a kick out of West Side Story. I wonder if they knew that West Side Story was really Romeo and Juliet in disguise.

Yea Albany Park had a subculture all its own. You knew who to talk to, and who not to talk to. You left certain girls alone, because either they were the sister of a gang member, or some gang dude was interested in them.

You even had comedians in Albany Park. There was a guy there named Cliff. He was very funny. I went to school with him. He would keep Albany Park laughing all the time. Cliff was a "rank-out" artist. If you tried to challenge him in the insults/put-down department, you were sure to lose. He would make fun of anybody, and since his brother Pint was in the Jolly Stompers, no one messed with him. I hear he is pursuing a career in comedy. I should have known. He was the comic in the park, like Bob was the comic on "the block."

The Hasidim! They never showed their face in Albany. Why? I don't know. I guess they thought there were too many black faces there. You see, they could confront us on "the block," because they could match up with us head-to-head. But the park had Blacks from all over the neighborhood. They were outnumbered, so they wouldn't dare come into Albany Park. They would stay outside, and peer through the fence. Who knows, some of those Jewish guys who stayed outside looking in might have been great basketball players. There might have been a Larry Bird in the bunch. But we never knew, because the Jewish parents definitely didn't want the Jewish kids mixing with us in the park. There were no ifs or buts about it.

If someone asked me if I think Albany Park helped or hindered us, I'd say it helped us. It "rounded us out." It brought the block guys closer to the gang guys, as well as the neighborhood athletes. The park introduced us to movies that premiered before we were born, and taught us about Hollywood, during its golden age.

We also learned a lot about Black Americans. Remember, I told you that most of us on the block came from the West Indian culture. The Black Americans in the park taught us about their culture and where their ancestors came from. Until I went to the park, I never knew what chitterlings were… or for that matter, peach cobbler. We also introduced some of the park regulars to curry goat, souse, and jerk chicken. So you see, we blended our cultures together at Albany Park.

We really blended when it came to the music. Music was a vital part of "the block" and Albany Park. To me, music put everything in perspective. I remember one instance when a James Brown song solved an altercation between two gangs. "The Payback" stopped a gang fight. Can you imagine that. The rhythm of that song made knives fall out of people's hands. The groove took over, and a prospective rumble turned into a dance rumble. But hey, things like that happened at Albany Park.

Chapter Seven

The Music

Brian O.

This chapter is devoted to music. "The block's" music. The park's music. The neighborhood's music. Music was a very important facet of "the block." When it comes to music, the letter "R" was very important around the block. Why, you ask? R & B, Reggae and Rap, though not necessarily in that order.

We ran the gambit of recording artists. From James Brown to Bob Marley. We grooved to a plethora of sounds. Hell, we even played the Beatles and Elton John. Those white boys had some serious lyrics. So did another... David Bowie.

In the early seventies, we were definitely into R & B. That's what was out at the time. The block played a "tug of war" between Motown, and the Sound of Philadelphia. On any given day, you would hear Stevie Wonder, Marvin Gaye, or the Temptations. Then, on the next day, you'd hear Harold Melvin and the Blue Notes, MFSB, Billy Paul... or Barry White.

There was also a lot of James Brown. Why wouldn't there be. He's the Godfather of Soul. Bart was crazy over James Brown. He loved his music, but could never sing the words right. He had no concept of the lyrics... but he sure knew the tune. Winston was an Earth, Wind, and Fire guy. He loved them. Bob loved Kool and the Gang, and Burt loved the Ohio Players.

Larry was the opposite of Bart. He knew the lyrics, but never knew who actually sang the song. Bart's buddy Claude knew who sang every song, but couldn't sing a lick. He had a bad stammering problem. Todd only liked one song... "Love is the Message." Whenever there was a party, that's the only song he'd get up and dance to.

As the seventies progressed, we all rode the disco wave. I think we were into every disco group except the "Village

People." I know I couldn't stand them. But we all loved Donna Summer, Heatwave, The Tramps, and First Choice. Me, I loved two singers especially: Candi Station and Loletta Holloway. Their songs really kicked. I especially loved Holloway's "Hit and Run"; and where would the seventies be without the Jacksons. To me, you should have called them "the Stalwarts." Every time you thought they were finished, they came back even stronger. When the disco era came in, they came up with killer tunes such as "Dancin' Machine" and "Blame it on the Boogie." Just before Michael went on his own, they scored big with "Heartbreak Hotel."

By the end of the seventies, "the block" was grooving to a guy named Prince. He scored with "I Wanna Be Your Lover" and "Sexy Dancer." After hearing those two "jams," we knew this guy was going to be something special.

And what can I say about those slow jams. Unlike today, where every song is crass and borderline vulgar, our slow jams were polished and classy. To this day, I can still hear Winston trying to sing "reasons" by Earth, Wind, and Fire. Was that a classy tune or what!! Me, I thought the Kings of slow jams were the Isley Brothers. Songs like "Livin' for the Love of You," "Voyage to Atlantis," and "Between the Sheets" gave them the title. If the Isley Brothers were the kings of slow jams, then the princes of slow jams definitely had to be the Stylistics. I mean, which one of you could argue that "Break up to Make Up" didn't send your hormones into orbit.

Now there are other R & B groups that deserve honorable mention. In the slow jam category, we gave props to DeBarge and the Moments. We also loved the Manhattans and Blue Magic. When it came to up-tempo dance tunes, we grooved to Brass Construction, Chic, The Crown Heights Affair, and B. T. Express. By the way, all of these groups, with the exception of Chic, came from good 'ole Brooklyn.

By the time the eighties came, we were ready for a change; and change was on the music horizon. We played snippets of Reggae in the seventies, especially Bob Marley and Jimmy Cliff.

But the eighties would see the "rise of reggae," and the phenomenon known as Rap/Hip Hop.

Around 1980, Winston's brother Rudolph moved up here from Jamaica. He helped to bolster our knowledge of Reggae.

Like I said, most of our families came from the Caribbean. So we heard the tunes. Some were Calypso, some were Reggae. We also knew the artists. But being in New York, I guess we put Reggae and the rest of the Caribbean music on the "back burner." It wasn't something that was intentional, it's just that we were being bombarded with American tunes. Rudolph changed that. While we were showing him how to play basketball, he was schooling us on the "Reggae Riddims." We taught him how to make a "hook shot," and he introduced us to Yellowman. We taught him how to get around the neighborhood, and he played his Bob Marley collection for us. One hand washed the other... so to speak.

After we got into Reggae, we grooved to the sounds of Yellowman, Beres Hammond, Gregory Issacs, and "Eeek-a-Mouse." We couldn't get enough of them. Reggae was a refreshing change from the disco/R & B. It also kept us in touch with our roots... most of us anyway. We would sing tunes from morning till night. Two songs I really loved were Bob Marley's "Is This Love" and Gregory Issacs'

"Night Nurse." And you know what? Our parents got more into the reggae than the R & B. They didn't mind our listening to Reggae. They could identify with it. Most of our parents would turn their noses up on R & B. With very few exceptions, they called it "Jungle Music."

Now if the parents despised most of the R & B, they really hated Rap music. But we loved it. After all, the origins of Rap came from part Reggae, and part R & B. So why wouldn't we like it. To top it off, many of those R & B pioneers… like Kook Herc and Grandmaster Flash, have roots in the West Indies.

Rap, where can I start. I guess the best place to start is at the beginning. Now I can get technical, and mention "The Last Poets" of the 1960's; but I'm not going to. I'm going to talk about Rap from 1979 to the present. Now you hear a lot of things. You hear Bronx is the home of Rap/Hip Hop; and the Sugar Hill Gang made the first rap record… "Rapper's Delight."

But let me tell you something. Check the archives. The first rap record of the modern era, was the Fatback Bands' "King Tim the 3rd", and they were from Brooklyn… yea that's right, Brooklyn.

Now I'm not here to get into a "rap ownership" war with the Bronx. But it seems to me that those Bronx guys never ventured out of their borough. As I recall, Brooklyn was spinning records and rapping to the beat as early as 1974. Remember the West Indian Day Parade I spoke about earlier? Well that parade is in Brooklyn. It stretched about 17 blocks. On almost every corner of that parade, there were D.J.'s "cuttin' and scratching"; and "rappin" on the mike. And that parade has been going strong for about 30 years. Now this wasn't just a one-day thing. Brooklyn night clubs like Ecstasy, and Love People II, were flooded with D.J.'s and Rappers.

Guys like Don and Raul learned to D.J. from frequenting these clubs. Hell you think they went to the Bronx to learn their craft? The Bronx was too damn far.

And you know what else? The Bronx didn't start claiming Rap/Hip-Hop ownership, until Boogie Down Productions' first album around 1986. They said in one of their tunes that "Bronx is the home of Hip-Hop," and it just snowballed.

Now don't get me wrong, I'm not saying the Bronx wasn't there at Rap/Hip-Hop's beginnings. I'm just saying they weren't the only ones. Come on Bronxites, give credit where credit is due. Stop trying to hog all the Rap glory. And besides, with all the West Indians in Brooklyn from 1974 till now, and seeing that Rap is a derivative of Reggae and Dancehall, where do you really think modern-day Rap originated? Let's just say New York City is the home of Hip-Hop; and leave it at that.

Hip-Hop artists, what a breed!! They practically created a new culture. Talk, clothing, style, you name it. Hip-Hop has put its stamp just about everywhere.

Now if you talk to different block members, I'm sure they would tell you their favorite artists. The artists of today, I feel, are too one-dimensional. They all sound alike. Some of them try to step out of "the formula," but for the most part, it's all the same.

Me, I liked the rap stars circa 1984 to 1988. Guys like Rakim, Slick Rick, and Big Daddy Kane did it for me. Those guys were original. They had a gimmic. I also dug Biz Markie, Kool G-Rap and my man Chubb Rock. Heavy-D was cool too.

When it came to groups, give me Public Enemy any day. Call them the "rap vaudevilleans." They even had comic relief. Where would the rap world be without Flava Flav. I also liked The Fat Boys, Run-DMC, The Fearless Four, and those gangster rappers from "Cali," N.W.A. The Treacherous Three, and the Funky Four plus One deserve honorable mention. They stood their ground with the "big boys".

You also have the "rap oddities." These guys succeeded in this genre, but for the life of me, I don't know how. They gave us no lyrics that you'd repeat ten years from now, but somehow they lasted in the Rap game.

When I think of rap oddities, the first person who comes to mind is "The Fresh Prince." How the hell did he do it? Good management I guess. Then again, he had D.J. Jazzy Jeff backing him up... and that dude was talented. The Fresh Prince might have been the most sensible rapper though. He parlayed his rapping into mega-millions on the movie screen. In that sense he's a visionary, and you can't fault him for that. While the other rappers wanted to be "bad boys," the Prince kept a clean image. I guess that's what the corporate world, and White America likes to see: a Rapper who is not threatening. Someone who will not stir up the masses. The Fresh Prince himself said a while ago, that he wished he had the courage to Rap, and use lyrics like Biggie Smalls. But I'm telling you he would never do it, because he knows what "side his bread is buttered on."

Another oddity of Rap was this dude called "Kwame"... with his "Sickening Polka Dots." Where the hell was he coming from with that nonsense. On the block, he was the Rap "whipping boy." Finally, my third rap oddity comes from an unlikely place... California. The reason I say this is because California had to play catch-up in the Rap game. So the "Rap gods" out there made sure everything coming from them was "banging." But to me, one guy slipped through the cracks. Oh he has a good following, but to me and most of the Block guys, he Raps like waste material. I won't use the "S" word. Guess his name yet? Well I'll tell you... it's Ice-T. What a crock. I guess of all the Rap oddities, The Fresh Prince is the best one. What the hell, he's from Philadelphia... very close to New York, so I'll put him down.

When you talk about Rappers before 1984, you're talking about the Rap Pioneers. Guys who paved the way. My favorites were Kurtis Blow, and Grandmaster Flash and The Furious Five. They had a world of originality, and Kurtis Blow had early crossover appeal. Who can forget "The Breaks!!" I also liked Africa Bambaata and the Soul Sonic Force. Run-DMC also goes in this category. They had the most staying power. Even Caucasian Rappers get mentioned in my book. I'm not prejudiced. My favorites were 3rd Base and The Beastie Boys. To hell with Vanilla Ice. The Block thought he just "looked corny."

The new Rappers come on the scene around 1989/90 to the present. New Rap standouts to me, are Busta Rhymes, Tupac, and of course, Brooklyn's own "Notorious Big"... Christopher Wallace; the great Biggie Smalls.

Let me give you my views on Tupac Shakur and Biggie Smalls. Though one was small and the other big, they both were the same when it came to one thing... "stirring up the Rap masses." Each of them had a strong following... still do. I always wondered why they never got together, put aside their differences (if they had any), and put Rap/Hip-Hop further into orbit. Now being from Brooklyn, I was always partial to Biggie. I thought he was the better

Rapper. But that's not the point. Costello was funnier than Abbott, Dean Martin sung better than Jerry Lewis (though Lewis was funnier), and Hope was definitely funnier than Crosby (though Crosby was the better singer). But what I'm getting at, is that these guys needed each other. Together they all "blew up"... and became large. If Tupac and Biggie forgot their "so-called differences," <u>boy</u>! they would have been larger than they were. In unity with these two guys, there would've definitely been strength. All I can say is, I hope each one of them finds unity and peace in the "afterlife." They both deserve it.

Rap females... naw, I didn't forget y'all. Though as a group the female Rappers were smaller, they still packed a wallop. The block gave props to MC-Lyte, Queen Latifah, Sha-Rock (from the Funky Four Plus One), and Salt and Pepa. With a modern day boost from Lauren Hill... female Rappers will be here for a long time. Foxy Brown, 'Lil Kim and Eve... to me and the rest of the block... the jury is still out on you. But stay strong, and you just might make it.

Finally, I've got to talk about what the block considered smash hits. Songs that were drop-dead chart toppers. The list goes as follows: "Heartbeat" by Tanya Gardner; "Love Thing" by First Choice; "Love Injection" by Trussel; "Got to be Real" by Cheryl Lynn; "Before I Let Go" by Frankie Beverly and Maize; "Keep in Touch" (Body to Body) by Shades of Love; "Funky Sensation" by Gwen McCrae; "Bounce, Rock, Skate, Roll" by Vaughn Mason and the Crew; "Grooveline" by Heatwave; "I Can Understand It" by New Birth; "Another Man" by Barbara Mason; and Brooklyn's own D-Train with "You're the One For Me."

I guess you can tell that I like music huh! All I can say is that music was one of "the block's" number one essentials. Still is.

Brian O.

Chapter Eight

The "Blackout"

Brian O.

You can't talk about "the block" without referring to the famous "Blackout" of 1977. Quite simply, it was an event. Lightning struck a main electric transformer, and that was it… The lights went out in New York City.

A singing group called the "Tramps" sang "Where Were You When The Lights Went Out in New York City." It was a long title, but a real funky tune. A "Disco hit." Part of that song said… "population's gonna grow, in nine months or so… where will all the little babies go." Incidentally, a lot of babies were born in April and May of 1978; just check the records.

Where were we? For the most part, right on the block. Remember, I told you, most of us had West Indian parents. They mandated that we stay put. Even wild and happy-go-lucky Burt stayed on his porch, and showed "porno films" in the street. He really had an audience that night…and a lot of batteries.

Most of us guys played games like "spades" and dominoes under candle light. Others tried to pair off with the girls. Bart wanted to play football. He thought playing in the dark would be fun. Andy was shooting pictures… of what I don't know. Pat was tinkering with something. I wonder how he saw what he was doing. And Bob? What else would Bob be doing… telling jokes. We had a battery-operated radio. So music was no problem. So we "chilled." We kind of fiddled… while Rome burned, so to speak.

All we saw that night were fires in the distance. We also heard a lot of gunshots, and some screaming.

The few that did venture off the block came back to report about the "urban war zone." If you wrote a poem about the blackout, you would have to call it "Looting and Shooting." Kyle and Lonnie reported that they saw two guys with two refrigerators on their backs, running down Utica Avenue; a major thoroughfare in our neighborhood.

All the girls stayed on the block. Even Joan... "the leader" stayed put. She could have ventured off, but I guess she wanted to show a good example to the others. And let's face it, it would have been a lot more dangerous for young ladies to be walking the street.

Every store imaginable got broken into. Bike Shops, Food Stores, Music and Appliance stores, you name it. After the blackout, everybody had new bikes, clothes, sneakers, etc. And you didn't have to loot items to have items. They were just laying anywhere and everywhere. If I remember correctly, that's how I owned my first radio cassette player. I saw it laying in a box at the corner.

Local politicians were driving around in a car, with a megaphone, urging people to keep calm. Now what sense did that make. They couldn't see where they were driving, and caused more harm than good. They wound up running into parked cars and street lamps.

Yea lawlessness, that was the name of the game during the Blackout of '77. It's amazing what citizens will do when they know they can get away with something.

Some store owners however, were very bold. They were determined that no one was going to break into their establishments. Many store owners stood outside of their shops with shotguns. The rioters left those stores alone. I guess they figured free items were not worth dying over.

And to top it off, with all that was going on that night, there was a mad killer on the loose; terrorizing couples who were in lovers' lanes all throughout the city. His name? David Berkowitz... the "Son of Sam". This guy spent that summer sneaking up on couples parked in cars, and blowing their brains out. Now I hate to say this, but the only thing the Black communities of New York City had going for them that night, was that the Son of Sam was targeting white people. This is one of the few times in American History, that Black people weren't being persecuted.

Now the "Son of Sam" had a Jewish last name. That didn't sit too well with the block's Hasidim. When the subject of "Son of Sam" came up, the Hasidim got irate. They didn't want to talk about it. I guess they figured they fit into the category of the people that were stalked, and were embarrassed that the "Son of Sam" might be Jewish. Anyway you put it, the Jews hated even the mention of this guy's name. It was like saying "Heil Hitler."

Yea the "Son of Sam" helped make the blackout unforgettable. But you know what? During the night of the blackout, the "Son of Sam" stayed put. You didn't hear a peep out of him. I predicted that you wouldn't… you know why? It's quite simple. The lights were out. No one could see where they were going. If this man tried to stalk on that night, he would have surely been captured. How could he have seen what he was doing? It was hard to see, so he would not have gotten a good look at his victims of choice. Also, his getaway would have been thwarted due to lack of vision.

Anyway, thank God he got captured approximately one month later.

If you think the blackout was not a serious issue, consider this: would you like to be blind for one night? I don't think so. Not being able to see is no joke. That blackout made me understand the plight of the blind… well somewhat anyway.

People being trapped in subway cars, looting, shooting, and screams were everywhere. The New York City Fire

59

and Police Departments were very busy that night. So were local hospital emergency rooms. I guess they treated the sick and injured by flashlight and candles.

I admired all the parents of "the block" that night. They set an edict, and put it into effect. No excuses. They performed their parental duties well. I guess they never figured a blackout would be in their "parental tenure." How could they? I guess being in a blackout is similar to being in a hurricane or earthquake. They say a major crisis brings out the best in people. It definitely did that night.

Will a blackout ever happen again? Who knows! The City said they have failsafe measures to make sure it doesn't happen again. But they said that in 1965, after the first blackout.

Chapter Nine

An Education…?

Brian O.

What constitutes a proper education? Why is education so important? Just how much education should one person have? These are the questions that have plagued parents and their children for years; and it was no different on... "the block."

Being immigrants, most of our parents ran that now famous line: "I want you kids to have a better education than we had." "You have all the opportunity in this country."

Were they right? Yea, they were right; but to a certain extent. I say this because no matter how much education one of my block mates acquired, he still had to deal with "the skin color factor." Let's face it, in corporate America or the Civil Service, there's just so far you're going to go being a minority.

And don't tell me about rich blacks like Oprah Winfrey or Bill Cosby. They had it hard, too. Their perseverance and "stick-to-it-ive-ness" got them where they are today. If they were white, they would have gotten there a lot faster.

Education is a wonderful thing. It opens your eyes to a lot of different avenues. I would advise anyone to seek sufficient education, because you're not going to make it in these United States... or the World for that matter, without one.

But don't let education blind you to reality. If you're a minority, be prepared to have some disappointments along the way. The best example I can give comes from Spike Lee's movie "Jungle Fever." The movie's central character was a black architect, who practically put this architectural firm owned by two whites "on the map." The two white guys promised him a partnership in the firm after a certain period of time; then reneged when the time came. His education could not hide his skin color.

Practically all the guys and girls on "the block" had some sort of education. The parents wouldn't want it any other way. Some of them were educated, and they wanted better for their children.

Some guys on the block had a vocational education. Kyle and Pat were good with their hands. Pat would tinker with radios and appliances; and Kyle would tinker with cars. Vinny had a brother named Richie who was also an "automotive head." Richie could fix anything that had to do with a car. Raul from Flatbush was also an "automotive head." He also tinkered with computers and stereo equipment.

Others on the block were into academia. They prided themselves on their grades and how far they got in school.

Some were into both. I guess those were the ones that wanted a "well rounded" education. I think I fitted into this category. I know Bob and Larry did.

One guy in particular Burt, had all the smarts in the world. He knew everything. He was a history and a mathematics nut; and he was good with his hands. The only thing he didn't excel in was English. But so what! We understood him anyway. But do you know what? He never went to school. He was the block's chief hookey player. Burt would hide out in a garage until his mother went to work and then go right back home to bed. Burt preferred a street education.

Let's face it. There were a lot of things we learned on the street. Some were good. Some were not so good. We learned how to shoot dice and gamble. We also learned about other races and their cultures; and we also learned about drugs, and "the fast buck."

Would I have traded in "my type" of education for another? I don't think so. I shudder to think about what my education would have been like if "the block" was in, say... Montana. Then again, I guess people in Montana say the same thing about us.

Education is important for the simple fact that you can always utilize it when you need to. I try to stress that to all of the youngsters nowadays. Having an education along with something else... let's say some kind of talent, makes a world of difference. It's always better to have than to have not.

Education can also make you stupid and crazy. Ever hear of people with book sense but no common sense? Or people that study so much they turn mad?

When it comes to education... like Clint Eastwood says, "you've got to know your limitations." Don't take on something if you know deep down it's not for you. If you know you're not disciplined, then don't go to college. Most of the block characters felt college was for the disciplined, not the smart. You could be smart in the Army... or in a trade school. When a person realizes what he likes to do and pursues it, that's what I call the beginnings of a sound education.

Why fool yourself! Doing something you really don't want to do makes a person miserable. If you study something because your parents want you to, you're not going to be happy.

Bob has a great education. But he realizes that comedy is something he wants to do. He worked with New York City Transit for years... and was miserable.

Me, I'm just realizing that I like to write. Who knows, maybe I'll be the next Steven King. If not, so what! It's something I like to do.

65

After being a New York City policeman for several years, Larry realized that he would rather be a lawyer, and is now pursuing his dream.

After dropping out of college, Boris realized that he needs that degree to move up at his place of employment.

Winston, Orlando, and Rudolph used their combined educations to open a business in Florida. They decided to strike out on their own. I guess they couldn't take the prejudices of the so-called "job establishment." Having an education made them realize they could work for themselves. God bless 'em.

Education!! What an important facet of life. It can make you or break you. I must say that it broke no one on "the block." You know why? Because we realized that education cannot take the place of friendship and comradery; and why should it! Why can't a plumber talk science with a doctor? Why can't an electrician discuss the law with a lawyer?

On many occasions, a doctor finds himself marrying another doctor. I understand why they do it. But once, just once, I'd like to see a doctor marry a home care attendant. Just once, would I like to see them look past their education and marry someone because they are a good person.

Is education so strong that it dictates our social mores? Is that now the norm? Better yet... can someone off "the block," be he Hasidic or Black, use the so-called "adequate education," to get him (or her) elected President of the United States? I don't think so.

And think about this. We were all taught to believe that your "vote counts." It was drilled in our heads from the time we were five years old. We were educated, and taught to believe that voting was the right thing to do. We were told that Black people died for the right to vote. So what happens? Along comes the year 2000, and the man with the most votes for president loses. The man who spent the most money during the campaign wins. The state that puts "Mr. Moneybags" in the White House and starts the vote controversy, is run by this brother. The Electoral College proves controversial and is in disarray. People are crying out for change. This country educated us into this system, and now descendents of some of those educators are trying to educate us out of this system. They are calling for change... voting reform. A change in the system. Education, for better or worse, will have the final say. Go figure.

Brian O.

Chapter Ten

The Language

Brian O.

Former New York City mayor David Dinkins once referred to "the gorgeous mosaic." Well if there were ever a "gorgeous mosaic" on "the block"… it was the language.

The language was from a broad spectrum. On one end you had a variety of West Indian Patois, on the other end you had the American South; with Yiddish stuck in between. Throw in good 'ole Pig Latin, and our language was a fascinating mix.

Now where else could I begin, than with the West Indian dialects. You heard it everywhere. You had the Jamaicans, with their own colloquials. They practically had their own language. Certain words they said were uniquely theirs… and no one elses. Some Jamaicans talked very abrasively, while others talked more refined. But they all knew what each other were saying; and when they argued the whole block could hear. When most Jamaicans want to get his or her point across, they don't care who's listening. I guess they figure why should they… they are not arguing with the people listening.

Yea that Jamaican vernacular was something else. Words like "T'raatid," "ras," "fi," and "chau" was strictly theirs. Being from a Jamaican family made me hear those words every day. And you know a funny thing about some Jamaicans? They would speak their language to no matter who they spoke to. If they were arguing with a Jew, they would argue and curse in the Jamaican lingo.

The Jews never knew what to say, or how to respond.

Next up to bat… were the Barbadians; or Bajans as they liked to call themselves. Bob's family was Bajan, and so was Vinnie's. They lived right next door to each other, and shared the same driveway. That area of the block should have been called "Bajan Central Station." It was ground zero for the Barbados contingent. Boy did you hear some slang around there; and it was entertainment.

You see, Bayans have that "sing song" type of accent. They are beautiful to hear. They talk like a never-ending sentence; very convoluted. But for some reason or another, you can understand what they're saying. And they have their own set of words, too. Words like "duz," "shite," and "botsie" are strictly theirs. Bob's older sister Sharlene, had one of the best Bayan accents I've ever heard. Unlike Bob and the rest of his brothers and sisters, she was born in Barbados, and lived there for a while. So her language was genuine.

Our block even had Spanish speaking West Indians. We had people from Cuba and Panama. Larry's mother being from Cuba, spoke beautiful Spanish. Her friend across the street Ms. Savon, also came from Cuba. These two women were unique because although they spoke Spanish, they sounded Jamaican. But that's understandable because of Jamaica's close proximity to Cuba, and the fact that people from those two islands mix and mingle with each other like crazy. Panamanians also mix with Cubans and Jamaicans.

Then we had families on the block whose heritage came from the American South. They had a language all their own also. Bart and Sal's family was from the South. Words unique to them were "y'all," "nu-in (nothing)" and "fetch me." I never heard them say "reckon" though. I only heard that on television.

The Southerners on our block were very quiet and polite. If they ever argued, we never heard them. They did however like to "spin a lot of yarn." There was a guy on our block named Mr. Duffy. He always had a story to tell about his experiences in the South; and he had an answer for everything. A real Mr. Know-it-all. But he was a lot of fun. If he bought a piece of candy for his kids and you were hanging out with them at the time, he'd buy one for you too. He was very generous.

At one time, we even had a Haitian family on the block. Now you know they had their own language. They didn't mix with the rest of us much. I guess they figured we wouldn't be able to understand them. They lived next door to Larry. So that part of the block had a Spanish/French flavor. Aah!! those romance languages.

Yiddish/Hebrew was another language that floated all over the block. You heard that in abundance. We had a synagogue on the block, so you heard Yiddish chants every Friday at sundown, and all day Saturday. The Jewish families would also hang out in "packs," and get into heavy conversations on the street. What were they talking about? As my mother used to say "only God knows." Sometimes I think they were talking about us. I could have sworn I heard a Yiddish version of "the N word" from time to time. Can't prove it though.

Hell, we even had Italians on "the block." There was "Paulie" with the stickball bat; and Tony who ran the neighborhood tattoo parlor. We heard a lot of "yoose," "fuggetaboutits," and their famous phrase "what am I, a moron?"

Then we had the infamous "Pig Latin." What would the block, or any neighborhood in New York City be without Pig Latin. That was our own language. No one else knew Pig Latin but the kids. Not the parents, not the Jews, not anybody. "Pig Latin" is where we struck back. We could say anything to anybody without repercussion. We couldn't talk it to gang members though, because they knew what we were saying. Hell, they were young too.

Brian O.

We all learned it from the same sources... school and the streets.

In Pig Latin, you kind of reverse the syllables of a word and add "ay" to the end. An example of this would be... alkin-tay for talking. That's a simple example, but it gets more intricate and difficult as the words get bigger, and you try to form sentences. Also, if a word started with a vowel, you really had trouble. Add to the fact that some Pig Latin on the block was combined with good 'ole West Indian Patois, and what was heard was really unrecognizable.

Languages, where would "the block" or the neighborhood be without them. They gave a style to the block and it's surroundings. When you heard the language of "the block," you knew you were in Crown Heights; or East Flatbush. You would never hear "our kind" of language in let's say, Bensonhurst. Only one language over there,... ditto Brighton Beach. That's Little Moscow. I bet you wouldn't find a "Roti" over there, either.

My block and others around it, had the gorgeous mosaic when it came to language. As soon as we walked around the corner to Empire Boulevard, we heard a lot of "Trinis" (Trinidadians) and Grenadians. What a melting pot.

Now Bob, being the comedian that he was (and is), used to try to create his own language, mixing together all the West Indian dialects and vernaculars. You'd have to hear it to believe it.

And we had our own words also. I won't tell you what they mean, but here are some just to name a few. "Trout," "buzzard," "wax," "Robert Newhouses," and "tietulas." Okay, I'll tell you one. If you say a girl has nice "Robert Newhouses," that means she has nice big thighs. We got this name from Robert Newhouse, a running back for the Dallas Cowboys in the seventies. He was very squatty, and apparently very strong. But what made him unique, was the fact that he had extremely huge thighs for his height and frame; thus the slang "Robert Newhouses." Ingenious isn't it. You see, guys on our block can think too.

Brian O.

Chapter Eleven

The Cuisine

Brian O.

What would the block be without its cuisines. Delicacies and treats that make your mouth water just thinking about them. Well we had many different dishes to sample from… from many different places.

And when we didn't get the specialty dishes from each other's homes, we had Chinese restaurants all over the area. Some of us also frequented Jewish bakeries. I know Burt did. He'd eat anything that wasn't nailed down. Like I said, he was daring.

The meals that we were exposed to were palate pleasing. Let's see, where do I start! Let's start with the Jamaican meals. They were spicy and delicious. Jamaicans have a thing for spice… especially pepper.

Whenever we ate at a Jamaican's home, we had dishes like Jerk Chicken, Curried Goat, Stewed Peas and Rice, Ackee and Saltfish, Pepper Shrimp, Rice and Peas, and Jerk Pork. The Jamaicans made great drinks too. Drinks like Carrot juice, Sour Sop juice, and Sorrel were "out of sight."

The Bajans had good food, too. They made dishes like Souse, Cou-Cou, and Flying Fish; and they made amazing fruit juices, and Mauby.

In Cuban homes, it was their black bean soup. What a treat!

When we ventured into a Trinidadian home, we ate Roti and Pelau. They were also heavy into curry and the fruit juices; and they made salads that were out of this world.

Remember I told you we had a friend from East New York called Carl. He was Guyanese. He introduced us to a lot of Guyanese delicacies; and boy did they have a lot. I remember meals such as Pepper Pot, Cook-up Rice, and Pineapple Tarts.

Also, meals from all the islands had some kind of way they prepared, spiced and served fish.

Some islands served a lot of steamed fish, some served fried. Some islands even baked fish. Jamaicans made "fish tea."

Bajans, as I mentioned earlier, prepared a meal called "flying fish." My favorite? "Escouvitch" fish. It was a spicy fish meal, with a lot of pepper, onions, and vinegar. Escouvitch had other spices also. Originally, I thought the Escouvitch Fish meal was a meal that originated in Jamaica. I guess that was because of my Jamaican heritage. Later on, I learned other islands had the same meal, they just called it something different. And they all made soups.

And talk about baked goods, cakes and desserts! The island meals were full of them. The Guyanese had Pine Tarts, Channa, and Carrot Cake. The Bajans made "Bakes" and all kinds of puddings.

The Jamaicans made Bread Pudding, Gizzardas, and Fruit Cake. Grenadians had a thing called "Blood Pudding."

It always seemed to me that West Indians could make a meal out of anything edible, that God put on this earth.

Like I mentioned earlier, the block's cuisine wasn't limited to just West Indian foods. Some of us experienced some Jewish foods also. It seems to me, that the Jews were heavy into baking. They baked a lot of cookies... especially this large one with one side chocolate and one side vanilla. I never knew the name of it... but it was good. The Jews also made loads of cupcakes and soups.

Now I'm sure their soups were good. But for some reason, I never partook in any of it. The soups always looked like something was alive, floating in it. I just wasn't going to take the chance. Some of our Jewish friends used to try and convince us that everything was all right… but most of us never tasted the soup. If I remember correctly, I think Burt drank it once. Yea their soup looked funny. I guess that's where Eddie Murphy got that "taste the soup" joke at the end of the movie "Coming to America." But there were a lot of Jewish delicatessens in the neighborhood and surrounding areas. Everything was "Kosher" this and "Kosher" that. On any given day on Kingston Avenue, you could smell corned beef and pastrami sandwiches all over the place. To some of us guys, knishes were as common as potato chips. And Jewish delis' made franks like "they were going out of style". There was no need for us to travel all the way to Nathan's; in Coney Island. Are you kiddin? The Jews also made some kind of meal out of "pita bread." It tasted okay too!

We even had Italian food in the neighborhood. There was a deli-grocery store called "Punzones" that made the best heroes in Crown Heights. They had calzones, pizza, chicken cutlets… the works.

Tony the tattoo guy and his goombahs used to frequent there all the time. The high school and junior high school kids in the neighborhood used to flock there also. What I remember about Punzones was their roast turkey hero sandwich. Later on they changed the name to Mama Louisa's, but the taste of the food has never changed.

And if we wanted ice cream, we would go to Taste of the Tropics. It was an ice cream parlor with exotic flavored ice cream. The ice cream flavors had a Caribbean flair. Flavors like Grapenut, Rum and Raisin, Egg Nog, Mango, and Sour Sop are flavors that were unforgettable.

We also had a place called Ice Queen. It wasn't actually in the neighborhood, but a short bike ride away. We used to jump on our bikes in packs, and peddle down to this place. It had the best Italian Ices in the world. Still does. What makes their ices so unique is that they have chunks of fruit in them; and they serve you a large quantity all the time. They never skimp. You don't mind paying them the money. Bart, Burt, and Bob used to bring home the biggest ices. They all had triple-decker jobs, and they would finish their ices by the time we got back home, and then bug the rest of the guys for some of theirs.

Our neighborhood also had fruit stands all over the place. Some fruit was domestic, some was imported. Some fruits were illegal, and were not allowed in the United States. I don't know how some fruit vendors smuggled these fruits in, but they were there. We actually had some fruits from our ancestral homes... or as some people would call it, "the old country".

I always thought that sampling cuisines from other places brought people closer, and made them more tight knit. I'll give you an example. Many West Indian islands made some kind of fried chicken. I myself was used to it one way. But I never really tasted fried chicken, until I went into the homes of my friends whose parents came from the American South. Their fried chicken was astonishingly good. So what did I do? I would ask let's say Bart's grandmother for her fried chicken recipe; get it, and give it to my mother. She would blend it with her recipe and make her chicken that much better. The same thing also happened in reverse. If my mother made something that Sal liked, he would get the recipe from her and give it to his mother. So you see, food brought many of our families together.

Yea, where would "the block" be without our neighborhood cuisines. Food was an integral part of our upbringing. Nowadays I only eat certain foods. A person's constitution changes as they get older. But I will never forget the time period when I could stomach all these goodies. Aah, youth... too bad it has to be wasted on young people.

Brian O.

Chapter Twelve

Sports

Brian O.

This chapter is devoted to sports. All kinds of sports. This book would not be complete, unless I told you about "the block's" view on sports.

Hell after our parents, I don't think anything influenced the guys on the block more... some of the girls too.

We grew up under the backdrop of many famous sporting events; and we all had our views on them. We all played high school sports, and some of us played in college. One of us even got a contract to play in the USFL.

Where do I start! Since this is America, let's start with the good 'ole American pastime... baseball. We all loved baseball. Some of us liked the Mets, some of us liked the Yankees. Me, I liked the Cincinnati Reds. "The Big Red Machine." Why do you say? What would a guy from Brooklyn be doing rooting the Cincinnati Reds! Well, it goes back to the year 1970. My public school took us on a class trip to see the Mets play. We were all excited. The season had just begun. It was either April or May, I don't remember. What I do remember was that after the game, we kids ran to the parking lot at Shea Stadium, to get a glimpse of the players leaving. It was the players parking lot. In those days things were less secretive. Players didn't secretly leave from some underground tunnel. Anyway, a bunch of Mets and Reds players came into the lot. We all ran up to them. We wanted autographs or handshakes or something. You know, not one Met acknowledged us that day. They just went into their cars. The Reds on the other hand were more cordial. Especially a guy named Bobby Tolan... and Pete Rose. Johnny Bench was also very nice. That day the Mets put a bad taste in my mouth and I've been a Cincinnati Reds fan ever since.

Pete Rose! Now there's a subject that stirs the emotions of the block. Love him or hate him, but you've got to admit one thing, he's being railroaded. The world wants him to admit to something he claims he didn't do. After a thorough investigation, then commissioner A. Bartlett Giamani promised he could be reinstated after one year. Within that years time Mr. Giamani dies, and the new commissioner gives "ole" Pete a lifetime ban; throwing in stipulations "after the fact." Pete Rose is told that if he just admits his guilt and apologizes, all **might** be forgiven. But I say why should he? Who can he trust? He was promised reinstatement and it fell through. Now you have suckers like sports announcer Jim Gray trying to squeeze an apology out of him. Pete never admitted to betting on Reds games; which was the most serious offense. And think about this! The only evidence they have against Mr. Rose is betting slip copies. Copies that have never been traced to anywhere. Why didn't a betting parlor or a bookie show up during the investigation? Stick to your guns Pete. Only you know the truth.

Another topic of block discussion is the famous (or infamous) New York Yankees. Love them of hate them, you gotta admit they are the most controversial team in the history of the sport. Me, I have nothing against this new crop of Yankess. But they are a far cry from the Yankees of old.

Now the Yankees are very successful. They have numerous World Series titles. I am not a Yankee basher. But I grew up in a family that hated the ground they walked on. Why?... because they had a great media machine. A player on their team... say Mickey Mantle would hit a mammoth home run; their announcers... especially Phil Rizzuto would say something stupid like "no one will ever hit a ball that far." Next thing you know, somebody like Harmon Killebrew would come up the very next inning, and hit the ball further out. Then Mr. Rizzuto would say "that's just a routine home run, the wind took it out." Shit, like that used to annoy me.

And as far as some of us guys were (and are) concerned, the Yankees only have about seven or eight legitimate championships. You know why? Because when the Yankees were winning prior to 1947, they were only playing with white ballplayers. There were no Black, Hispanic, Japanese, nothing. How can you test your skill if you're not playing against the best of all races. In the 1950's and early 60's, they only had a handful of minorities. So, those don't count either. I'll give them the 1970's championships and the 90's-2000 championships. That's it. When free agency came around, that really helped the Yankees. With the size of their market, they have no problem shelling out cash to get the best players. It's hard for a small market team to compete. But I guess if the Yankees weren't involved in something, they wouldn't be the Yankees. Whether it was Billy Martin's fighting and drinking or Stienbrenner's association with gambling. There's always something. One thing I'll say about George Stienbrenner though. He gives minorities a chance. He'll grab a prospect out of the Caribbean in a minute. Yea the Yankees!! They are the J.R. Ewings of baseball. Always up to something.

One thing I'll always remember when it comes to baseball, was the way Hank Aaron was treated as he neared breaking Babe Ruth's home run record. The only person who probably got worse treatment than him was Jackie Robinson. Guys like me, Bob, and Todd used to look at the evening news and sports shows in amazement. We couldn't believe a person's life was being threatened because he was about to break a sports record. After all, it's just a game. Records come and records go. Think about this! Society criticized that same Babe Ruth. They called him a whoremonger with a ravenous appetite. They said he partied too hard. They called him a glutton, and too stupid to manage. Hank Aaron on the other hand, was a gentleman. You never heard him getting into any trouble. He carried himself with dignity. So we have here a gentleman and so-called miscreant; and who does society persecute... the gentleman. Only in America.

Now another guy that stirs emotions is Curt Flood. He challenged the baseball gods. As far as "the block" and I am concerned, he created free agency in sports. Mr. Flood sued baseball, to challenge their unfair trading practices. His bold move paved the way for free agency in all major sports; which now allows players to have a say in their trades to other teams, and to negotiate competitive salaries. If it wasn't for Curt Flood, you wouldn't have all these multi-millionaire athletes today. And what did Curt Flood get for doing all this? Ostracized. From what I hear, he died a lonely and bitter man. I think major league baseball should name a stadium after him... or at least an award. You can say Curt Flood is another Jackie Robinson; because just as Jackie broke the color barrier in baseball, so did Curt break the sports "financial" and "slavery" barrier. I say slavery because before Curt, you had no say in where a team sent you. You were traded... like slaves or cattle. After Curt Flood this all changed.

Football is the next topic of discussion on my sports Odyssey. It's a sport we all loved. Most of the guys on the block (I could honestly say the majority), played organized football at some time or another. Be it sandlot, high school, or college, football was a part of us... like a body mole. Our block would challenge other blocks in the

The Block: A Brooklyn Story

neighborhood and beat them all. We would play on hospital grounds, parking lots, parks, anywhere. On Thanksgiving day before dinner, we would play a big game outside in the street. Man, it was a war. Of course Bart was always up to his shenanigans. Bob was running down the sidelines telling jokes. Todd? now that was a strange guy. He would play football in this winter coat called a "quarterfield." I don't know how he moved around. "Off the block" guys like Will and his brother Rods came to play too. Will was a neat freak. He never wanted to get dirty. I think Will had "tailor made socks."

Claude came also. Actually, Claude was the biggest guy of the bunch. But he was gentle. You had to get him really mad for him to fight. Bart knowing this, used to provoke him all the time. He used to put Claude in a "headlock" on many occasions. But when Claude got really mad, Bart would leave him alone. Well anyway, when we all got together, football was fun.

We also had our views on the NFL… especially some of the players. Let's see where do I begin. Oh Yea.. Franco Harris. He was a big topic of discussion on "the block." I could take him or leave him. But others such as Bob, Bart and Claude couldn't stand him. They said he ran out of bounds too much, and would never take a hit. I think Bob despised him especially, because of the "Immaculate Reception"! That famous play that beat the Oakland Raiders in the playoffs; in the seventies. You see Bob was a big Raiders fan. They could do no wrong for him.

Now let's talk about everybody's favorite football player… Walter Payton. "Sweetness." Was he a star or what! What was so special about this guy you ask? Everything. He wasn't the biggest guy. He wasn't the strongest guy. But he was the most dedicated. He had a

91

hell of a work ethic. And he first gained notoriety doing of all things... dancing. He danced on "Soul Train." Can you believe that. He was football's version of "Bruce Lee"; for Bruce was a dancer too. He was a Cha Cha champion. Well unlike 'ole Franco, Walter Payton never ran out of bounds. He took hits and he dished them out. I'll never forget that forearm of his whacking linebackers and safeties on top of their helmets. And Walter was another one who never created any controversy. He was a player on the field and a gentleman off. They say he was sort of a comedian also. If that's true, then that's something extra to like about him.

You all will never know how torn up Bob and I, and the rest of the block guys felt when he died. Of course I never knew him personally, but I think about him all the time. If Hollywood ever makes a movie about him, I'll be the first one in line to see it; and I'm sure wherever the guys are, they'll see it too. Damn, the good always die young.

Now you could never talk about football without mentioning the name of one O.J. Simpson. The block guys loved him. Hell the whole neighborhood loved him. Will used to wear a t-shirt which said "The Juice is Loose – 2003 yards." I had a poster in my room which said "The Electric Company Turns on The Juice." To my generation, O.J. was the first commercial superstar. He had a lot of endorsements. O.J. was the precursor to Michael Jordan. And boy, could he play. He had speed to burn. He never "juked" you like Walter Payton did. He just flat-out-ran you.

My impression of O.J. though, is of a guy who seemed to forget where he came from. I don't hate him, hell I don't even know him. But it seems to me that he let his "hat get away from his head"...if you know what I mean. His "business" it seemed, was always out in the street. Am I going to talk to you about his murder trial? NO! This is about sports. But if possible, some of the fellas and I would like to meet O.J. Simpson one day. Believe me, we have a lot of questions to ask him. Hell, he could eat right at my dinner table.

Joe Namath. Now there's a name that conjures up memories. He was flash. But he wasn't a "flash in the pan." What we liked about him was his style off the field. Broadway Joe, that's what they called him. Anybody who can predict a Super Bowl victory... and achieve it, is all right with me. And unlike Babe Ruth's so-called "called shot," which no one has any film of (and no proof – it's always portrayed in a drawing), Joe's prediction was the real thing.

You want basketball, I'll give you basketball. We all loved it. That game stirs many memories. Who can forget Walt "Clyde" Frazier, with his sleekness on and off the court. Who could forget Willis Reed's pain and triumph in the 1970 championship against the Lakers.

And then there were those dreaded boys from "Beantown," the Boston Celtics. Can you talk about New York basketball without mentioning them? I don't think so. And what about Earl "The Pearl" Monroe and Wilt Chamberlain? You can never forget those guys.

Sal used to pattern his game after Doctor J. He swore he was Julius Erving. And Orlando! He used to dribble the ball profusely, like he was "Tiny" Archibald... or Pistol Pete.

As the years passed, we got into the three main basketball players, synonymous with the eighties: Magic Johnson, Michael Jordan and Larry Bird. I could not write about basketball without mentioning these three. Who was better? That's your opinion. Personally myself, and most of the guys on the block thought it was Jordan. I called him the "Walter Payton" of the NBA. To me his tenacity and will to win, put him slightly ahead of the other two. Magic Johnson? What can you say about him. He could turn the fortunes of a team around, by just stepping on the court. The man had eyes in the back of his head. Bart thought he could pass the ball like Magic. Who was he fooling?

And Larry Bird? Who shot the ball like him? I mean this guy could shoot from behind the basket near the "out of bounds" area, and it goes in. He had lethal range. A shooter's touch. When he came to Madison Square Garden I felt sorry for the Knicks; because you always knew that some way or another, Larry was going to beat them. Oh Bernard King kept the game close, but in the end it wasn't enough.

Patrick Ewing. Now there's an interesting topic. Some of us loved him. Some of us booed him. Our feelings were mixed. In the beginning of his pro career, everybody loved Patrick. He came to the Knicks with high expectations. He started out like a "house of fire." Most of us wanted him to succeed because he was Caribbean. He represented the "what ifs" for the whole Caribbean region. Oh there were other Caribbean ballplayers; but none with the fanfare of Patrick Ewing. The first lottery pick ever. So what happened? I'll tell you what happened. Fans set his standard too high. Then he started to believe he was as great a player as fans said he was. Now I'm not saying he's a bad player. He's one of the best. But he never learned how to adapt to changing situations. If a guy like Walt Frazier can adapt to Earl Monroe's coming to the Knicks... then why couldn't Patrick adapt when other players came?

Now lately I've heard people say that Patrick didn't have the players around him to win a championship. Maybe that's true, maybe it isn't. But for the mere fact that he got to a championship, meant that he had a chance to win one. Great players have a strong mental game, especially when you reach the championship.

To some of the guys on "the block," Patrick Ewing did not make his teammates even slightly better. But hey... at least he made the NBA's top 50 players. Congratulations Patrick!!

Now I want to get into sports figures from any sport, who we block guys loved. First off, you have John McEnroe. He's a regular "walk-it-like-he-talks-it" type of guy. He could hang out with us guys any day. Then there's Arthur Ashe. He was class personified. Then there's Tiger Woods. He is more recent. But "the block" guys love him. He is revolutionizing golf, the way Bill Russell and Kareem Abdul-Jabbar revolutionized their sport. And Jim Brown? What's there not to like about him?

Finally, the guys would kill me if I didn't conclude this chapter talking about one of our favorite sports... boxing. We all loved boxing. But no one ever took it up. Of course when you speak of boxing, the first person that comes to mind is... that's right you guessed it, Muhammed Ali.

Ali should be athlete of the century. Let me tell you why. Not only did he revolutionize boxing. But if he wasn't a fighter, he'd be a poet or an author. And he was a dynamic public speaker. He was at home in front of the camera. He could sing too. I'm sure he could have been a great movie star. And we adored him because he stood up for his beliefs. He said he didn't have anything against the Viet Cong? They never called him the "N" word? He's damn right. I wouldn't have fought either. One day, I heard someone on the TV say "Ali should have fought in Vietnam. Look what his country did for him. It made him rich." Yet this is the same country that discriminated against him after the 1960 Rome Olympics. He proudly wore his gold medal into a restaurant to get a bite to eat. They didn't serve him so he took off his medal and threw it in the river. He could win a gold medal for his country, but he couldn't eat in one of his country's restaurants. You think they would have done that to Joe DiMaggio? No way. All the guys on the block liked Ali. If you didn't, you lost your "hang-out card."

Then there was Joe Frazier. Ali needed him. Hell, they needed each other. Frazier came around at the right time. And he was tough, too. I've never seen a guy who could take so much punishment, and keep on coming. Frazier was made out to be the enemy of the Black community, because Ali was so popular. But I think he got a bum rap; and I think this <u>gnaws</u> at him to this day.

George Foreman? Everybody loved him too. For some reason, the parents liked George a lot. I don't know why. Maybe it's because he used to wear that "apple jack" hat. You see back in the seventies, a lot of West Indian guys used to wear that hat. Or maybe, it's because George Foreman won his first championship in Kingston, Jamaica.

But if George was loved by the West Indian community, he was not loved by many Black Americans. Sal's father didn't like him. I think this stemmed from the time when he waved the American Flag at the 1968 Olympics. We called them the "Black Power Olympics," because of Tommy Smith and John Carlos. George was seen as a white champion and the Black community was elated when Ali knocked him out, in of all places... Africa.

But Foreman was reborn. He became beloved. He regained his championship in the 1990's. He became a media darling. Now that's a Hollywood script.

Kudos go to Sugar Ray Leonard, Tommy Hearns, Roberto Duran, and Wilfred Benitez. These guys brought flair to the other divisions. Marvelous Marvin Hagler was another one. How could I forget him.

As for Mike Tyson, most of the guys like him too. You see, we feel Mike is the most misunderstood boxer in history. People take out of context everything he says; and Mike needs to surround himself with positive people. If he does he'll be the heavyweight champion again in no time. Go get that belt Mike.

Currently, all I do is reminisce about those big football games we used to have. We need to have one more game before we totally lose contact with one another. Maybe I'll put the bug in Bart's ear.

Brian O.

Chapter Thirteen

TV and Movie Favorites

Brian O.

I could never end this book without talking about the block's TV and movie favorites. TV shows and movies were the topic of discussions almost every day. We always had something to say about some show. I think the TV shows of the 1960's, 70's and 80's are ten times better than the shows of today. Even the soap operas were better back then.

When it comes to television, it seems "the further back you go, the better the show!" In the 90's, the "big" sitcom was Seinfeld. Now Bob being the comedian that he is, understands Seinfeld; and gets into it. But guys like me, Jasper and Orlando... we just don't get it. To us, Seinfeld is dry and corny. And don't tell me it's a Black/White thing, because all of us on the block went crazy over Archie Bunker and "All in the Family." That was a great show. Archie Bunker kept us in stitches all the time. His jokes and mannerisms were timeless. You can't compare Archie to Jerry Seinfeld. In our opinion, Archie would "blow Jerry out of the water"!

On our block we recognized good humor (and I'm not talking about the Ice Dream truck)... Black or White. It didn't make any difference what color the comedian was. We all loved Lucy, and were crazy over Ed Norton. We liked Jackie Gleeson too... he was hilarious. But Ed Norton was the man. He was "too" funny. I always said the people in Hollywood could have, and would have had a monster sitcom, if they paired Lucy and Ed Norton on a TV show; and let Jackie Gleeson and Desi Arnaz produce it. Can you imagine what kind of show that would have been?

Some of us guys also dug "Three's Company"... with Jack Tripper and the two girls. But what used to "piss us off" about that show was this! Chrissy and Janet never wanted to "get romantic" with Jack. But when he tried to

101

find romance elsewhere, the girls would attempt to thwart his efforts. In block vernacular, they were c__k blockers (readers can add in the letters if they like). Now that's not right.

Then there was "The Jeffersons." That was a great show. We loved it because it made Black people look positive; yet realistic. I'll tell you what I mean. TV viewers saw the gradual rise of George Jefferson. It started from "All in the Family." By the time The Jeffersons came along, he had already "moved on up"; as the show's theme song went.

Now let's compare the Jefferson's to the Cosbys'. The block loved the Cosbys'. It was another positive show. It showed how far people (of any color) can go with an education. But the Cosby show was somewhat unrealistic. Larry and I recognized this very early in the show's run. I'll tell you why. Cliff was a doctor and Claire was a lawyer right? To be a doctor takes years of studying; it's hard. To go the law school route and become a lawyer is almost equally as hard. The burning question remains... when did Claire have time to go to law school and become a partner in a law firm? She had five kids, and two of those kids were very young. Did she start law school right after college? Evidence on the show says no!! What evidence supports this? Cliff and Claire had a daughter in her 20's when the show began. Another girl was in her late teens, with a son one year younger. Did Claire have these three kids and raise them in a law school library? I don't think so. And don't tell me that it's possible, because Cliff had his practice in the basement. Hell, he was a Gynecologist/Obstetrician. What did he do! Tend to his young kids and women's privates at the same time? The bottom line is that Claire had five kids. That means she spent around 50 months, approximately four years in the state of pregnancy. I'm not even getting into the child rearing part of it. That would tack on more years. I guess I wouldn't be so skeptical if Claire was an elderly woman... say around sixty-five. But she was portrayed as someone in her early to mid forties. The show said Cliff and Claire married when they got out of college (undergraduate). Normally, that would put a person around twenty-one or twenty-two. Now look at the ages of those kids, and you do the math.

But, I'm not lambasting the show. Like I mentioned earlier, the block loved it. Except for my "knit picking," it was a very positive show. It showed what can happen when parents take an active role in their children's lives. The block could identify with this, because our parents took active roles in our lives.

On the "flipside," we had "the Evans family." Good Times. That's another show I'd like to discuss. After watching the Cosby Show and Good Times, I'd rather the Cosby Show. This is because Good Times was too depressing. I loved the characters – especially J. J. and Whillona. But I mean give me a break! Every opportunity they had to better themselves met with disaster. I remember the episode when Thelma was going to "make it out" because she married a star athlete. Everything was rosy. They were going to get settled in a big spread, then buy a big house for the rest of the family. Then all of a sudden, through horseplay, the athlete gets a career-ending knee injury; and winds up living in the Evans' apartment. Now I know bad luck could happen. Hell, Teddy Pendergrass made that perfectly clear in his song. But too many things happened to the Evans'. It's like one of them was wearing the "Hope Diamond." It seemed to me like the show was trying to tell Black people that they will never be able to improve on their current situations. For guys like Larry, Bob, Jasper, and Skeeter, that was kind of hard to swallow.

Especially Jasper, he was a very positive guy. I think somehow, Bobby McFerrin stole the "don't worry, be happy" phrase from Jasper. Nothing ruffled his feathers. Being positive can make a person go a long way. I guess the show Good Times reminded some people that we still have a long way to go.

Now without a doubt, the block's favorite show was Sanford and Son. I still think it is the best sitcom TV has ever produced. Bold statement huh! I don't care. I loved Sanford and Son and so did everybody on "the block." Why did we have such admiration for Sanford? Because Sanford was the real deal. There was nothing phony about that show. Fred and Lamont weren't rich, and they weren't poor; but they were comfortable. Just like George Jefferson, Sandford had his own business. We could identify with Fred Sanford, because there were junk and salvage businesses all over Brooklyn. It's an honest profession. You can make a lot of money in it. A junk collector is an "urban archaeologist" I see nothing wrong with that. If you find a ten carat diamond in the city and a ten carat diamond on some mountain, the results are the same. It's still a ten carat diamond. The comedy on Sanford and Son was great. Their episodes kept us guys and gals in stitches. And Sanford and Son had great characters too. Who can forget Aunt Esther and Grady. Or those freeloaders… Bubba, Leroy, and Skillet! Redd Foxx was a comedic genius. To me, he paved the way for future comedians.

Oh there were comedians before Redd, but none of them had the influence on younger comics like Redd did. Redd Foxx influenced the new generation of comedy. So did Richard Pryor. Let's not forget him. Pryor was an innovator. He was also ahead of his time. Like Lucy and Ed Norton, can you imagine what a Foxx/Pryor sitcom would be like? It would have been great. The only problem would have been ... who was going to play the straight man?

Movies? Where would "the block" be without them.

Unlike television, you could find a good movie and great actors, in any time period; be it the 30's, 40's, 50's, 60's, 70's, 80's, or 90's. Who can deny that they had some great actors back in the 30's, 40's and 50's. Guys like Bogart and Cagney, Raft and Robinson ruled the silver screen. They all had a loyal following. Which one was the best? That's hard to say. Bart loved Cagney, Todd loved Edward G. Robinson, Bob loved Bogart. Me, I loved them all. Each one of these guys could take over a movie. Bogart had his lisp; Cagney's body movements were legendary; George Raft's eyes could pierce a hole right through you; and Edward G. Robinson? His voice was something to behold. Can you imagine these four guys on "The Sopranos"?

Then there were the "Lover Boys." Guys like Clarke Gable, Tyrone Power, and Victor Mature. You also had those "four star" ladies. Actresses like Bette Davis, Joan Crawford and Grace Kelly filled the screen. Hell, back in the day, they even had the so-called "minority" actresses "lighting up" the screen. Gals like Dorothy Dandridge, Hattie McDaniel, Lena Horne and Ruby Dee were great.

And you know I can't leave out the "Pioneer Brothers." Guys like Sidney Poitier, Harry Belafonte, Paul Robeson, and Canada Lee, paved the way for the Denzels and Wesleys of today. Those guys were excellent.

Then you have the kind of actors that would be great in any era. Guys like Robert DeNiro, Al Pacino, Dustin Hoffman, Gene Hackman, Marlon Brando, Lawrence Fishburne, Morgan Freeman, Samuel L. Jackson, and Lou Gossett, could act no matter what decade it is. And even though Eddie Murphy is a comedian by trade, most of the block thinks he's a good actor. He doesn't act "hammy"… like Will Smith. Eddie is more natural. Another actor that I personally like is Sean Penn. He is very intense. He could go a long way in this acting business.

Now before I get away from myself, let's get into some of "the block's" favorite movies. We weren't into westerns at all. But if we had to pick two we enjoyed the most, they would have to be "Buck and the Preacher" and "Blazing Saddles." To many of us block guys, Blazing Saddles is one of the best movies ever made; if not one of the funniest.

Then we have our so-called "cult movies." These movies have a following. We block guys talk about them year in and year out. These movies will go down in "the block's" hall of fame. They are as follows: "The Godfather," Parts I and II; "Scarface," with Al Pacino; "Enter the Dragon," "King of New York," "Marked For Death," with Steven Segal; "Cotton Comes to Harlem," "One Flew Over the Cukoos Nest," and "The Warriors." Throw in "Die Hard" and "Jungle Fever," and you have the block's hall of fame cinema. If I forgot any, I'm sure "the block" will let me know after they read this chapter.

Chapter Fourteen

The Chances We Take

Brian O.

You know the saying "you live and learn." Well that saying definitely applied to "the block." Now in this chapter, I intend to keep things as anonymous as possible. You see, I respect people's privacy. What can I say! The chances we take can make us or break us. Lord knows, we took a lot of chances on "the block."

Let's see, there was the time when one of the guys took his father's new Mercedes Benz to his girlfriend's house; and got it stolen. He took forever to come home. When he did, boy was he ridiculed.

Then there was the guy who experimented with I.V. drugs. I mean he took drugs before, but in the age of HIV, this was not the thing to do. He did it anyway. Well the inevitable happened. Let's just leave it at that.

Why do we take chances? Because most youngsters think they are invincible. But I'm here to tell you that's just not true. Let me give you another example.

There was the time when one of the crew walked around with a gun. Well one day, miscommunications between this guy and the police led to his being shot five times; and gravely wounded. Could all of this have been avoided? Who knows! Once a firearm is so much as spotted anywhere near a black person, that's it. For some reason bullets begin to fly. Our homeboy knew this and took a chance walking around with that gun.

Here's another example. One of the guys... a very smart guy, went away to college. This guy could have gotten any degree he wanted; Bachelors, Masters, Ph.D; you name it. This guy's only problem was that his attention span varied easily. When my buddy got to college, he got into the fraternity life. Ain't nothing wrong with that. I know a lot of people who joined fraternities, and they still graduated from college. They didn't take it

Brian O.

too seriously. But my buddy did. As a result, he didn't graduate. I tell him all the time, he needs to finish college. Who knows, maybe one day he will.

You know there's a thin line between what might happen and what actually happens. Take for example, the time when two of us guys got run over by automobiles. We were kids, we thought we were fast. Then bang, we were hit. Did we take a chance? Yea, we did. Did it pay off? No, it didn't. But hey, that's life.

I mentioned in an earlier chapter that one of the guys had a chance to make it in pro football. He was good, and he knew it. When he got the pro contract, some of us guys told him to train and stop "hanging out"… living the "street life." We told him to put down the weed and the "Drog" (what we call alcoholic beverages), and the women, and concentrate on conditioning; and making the team. But our friend did just the opposite. Again being young, he thought he was invincible. As a result, he didn't' make the pros. Just think about it. He could have been big time. Now he's just a regular 9 to 5er.

Talk about 9 to 5… that's a big chance too!! Some of us were meant for 9 to 5, some of us were not. One of the guys used to bitch and moan about going to his job every day. It was far from "the block," and he wasn't getting any respect on his job. He was miserable, so what did he do? He "cashed his chips in"… and quit. Big chance right? But I'll tell you what… now he's working for himself, and he's very happy.

Another block guy had a brother who started college. That's what his parents wanted him to do. Like all "the block" parents, they preached that going to college was the right thing to do. But apparently, college and this guy couldn't see eye to eye. However, this guy was no fool.

He knew what he wanted. He always liked music, and when he went to college he hooked up with people in the music business. He met the right people and got his foot in the door. Now as they would say on the street, "he's big time." He has carte-blanche in the music business. He dropped out of college to pursue his dream; and it paid off. That's the chance he took. Would this have worked with another block guy. I don't know. But this one particular guy showed perseverance. I wish him all the luck in the world.

Yea some of us guys were risk takers. Sometimes, it's okay to take risks. But I feel you should take risks with a plan. Here's an example of one of the block guys who took a risk without a plan. This guy was sailing along in college. He didn't have much more to go. He could practically smell graduation. So what happened? He got involved in the selling of vacuum cleaners. My buddy got "souped up" by the hype. People at the vacuum cleaner company told him there was money to be made. They quoted millions. He fell for it. Took the bait. Dropped out of college. Then the vacuum cleaner business "dried up." No one wanted these expensive vacuum cleaners.

As a result, my friend was left "drifting" with no job; and an unfinished college education. And remember, once you quit college for an extended time period, it's hard to go back. My partner never did. His chance turned into a big zero. But hey, that's life.

I'm taking a chance writing this book. What am I doing this for? Do I think my book will make me tons of money? Will it fall into the hands of some famous Hollywood producer and be turned into a screenplay/movie? Will I offend some people by writing it? Who knows? It's a chance I've chosen to take.

Brian O.

Now one of our friends took a really big chance. This chance got him into all kinds of trouble. Let's see, where do I begin. Guess the first place I should begin is the college he chose to attend.

If I remember correctly, he got some kind of scholarship to play football; at some college in the Midwest. When he got out there, he told me all he saw was corn… and hillbillies. He said there weren't too many African-Americans out there.

But it was a scholarship, so I guess it was in his best interest to go there and utilize it. Anyway, when he got there, he started going out with one of the local girls. I don't know if it was "Jungle Fever" or what, but he fell for this chick. Well one thing led to another, and this girl got pregnant. Now whether he was forced to marry her or not… no one knows. But he did; finished his collegiate career, and brought her to Brooklyn.

In Brooklyn they settled into Bedford-Stuyvesant. Forget Harlem, Bedford Stuyvesasnt is the African-American capital of New York. The girl just didn't fit in. To top it all off, at times she would spew racial remarks at people. We put up with it, because she was married to one of our boys. But some of us didn't like it.

Well anyway, they had two more kids and I guess life was gravy. Then we had heard that drugs started to "raise its ugly head." Now I don't know who started taking drugs first, but all I know is that my friend was not a substance abuser until he met this chick.

Next thing you know, they were constantly bickering and fighting. I hear the wife was even involved with some drug dealings on her job. Soon they both started to sell their belongings. That's when you know recreational drug use has gone to the next level. Things started to spiral downhill for them. He wouldn't be seen for days at a time, and then all of a sudden, he'd pop up.

Well one day the "chain finally snapped"… so to speak. His wife was reported missing by her job. The police suspected foul play, and were looking for her husband, our homeboy! What the hell was going on we wondered. Later on she was found… dead… brutally dead; and I'll leave it at that. It was all on the news. The kind of "shit" you see on Murder, She Wrote! Only there was no Jessica Fletcher to solve this crime. No Columbo either. The NYPD put out an "All Points Bulletin" (APB) on "our boy."

When we finally caught up with him, he didn't speculate on what happened; and being the type of guy that he is we didn't ask him. He was very interested in the welfare of his kids but that was it. He said nothing about his wife, and no one pressed the issue. After all, most of "the block" guys never got into the domestic squabblings and situations of others. We were taught that by our parents.

Eventually, after a few days on the "lam," our friend walked into his lawyer's office… thus in effect, surrendering to police. Did our friend and block brother commit this act? Who knows!! If he didn't do it, does he know who did? Who knows!!

All we know is he's in jail right now, "doing time for the crime." Now I know whoever reads this will say "if he didn't do the crime, why is he doing the time"?

To that all I can say is unlike O.J. Simpson, my friend does not have deep pockets. He couldn't afford Johnny Cochran. Maybe he knows something about the crime but is not telling; and as a result has to do the time. Or maybe he's taking the fall for somebody. Like I said before… who knows!!

Brian O.

But I do know this! The chances he took led him to his current predicament. The choices also. Why did he have to travel miles away to attend college? Was the school he got the scholarship from better than any of the nearby colleges... no!!! If he never went there in the first place, he'd have never met that girl. But let me not be too critical. That's hindsight!! Because he could have gone out there and found the perfect woman. Anyway, through thick and thin, he's still my partner. "The block" doesn't give up on one of it's own so easily. Because we feel a chance taken shouldn't destroy a lifetime of friendship.

Chapter Fifteen

Epilogue

Brian O.

Well what else can I say about "the block," that has not been said already. A lot of things. I just scratched the surface. I could tell you that all of us "lived happily ever after," but that would not be true. This isn't a fairy tale. It's a reality tale; in short story form.

Most of the guys and gals grew up to have kids and families of their own. Some moved out of the New York City area, and a few met with untimely deaths. Some have battled back from drug abuse, some haven't.

Some went the military route. Others became successful doing other things… such as writing, comedy, and opening up their own businesses. Our block has a very diverse crew.

Me? I'm an exterminator. Ain't that a pip? What is an exterminator doing writing about the chronicles of a block? Hell I've heard of stranger things… like a school teacher taking a ride in a Space Shuttle. That didn't work for her… maybe writing will work for me.

It's the new millenium, and the block has changed. Most of the guys come back to reminisce. The gals too. We've lost track with some of the crew. Others are in situations where they can't come back.

Some parents are still there. Some have moved to places like Florida and the Carolinas. Some are no longer with us. They have completed earth's curriculum, and have graduated to the heavens. God bless 'em.

Yea the block has totally changed. There's no more football and "punch" ball games. We played "punch" ball like we were in Yankee Stadium. I don't see the new kids playing Ring-O-Livio or RCK (Run, Catch, and Kiss). There's nothing going on. Even the Jewish kids don't play outside anymore. Back in the day they would play in their driveways. Some of them would even play with us. Now you barely find one or two of them playing outside.

I did see some Jewish kids playing in Albany Park the other day. Now that's new. Back in the day, the Hasidim didn't go in there. That place was off limits to them. Now they're in Albany frolicking… what a change.

I remember when the weekend came, I guess it was after sundown, the Jewish families couldn't turn on or off a stove; or touch anything electric. They would call us into their homes to perform these tasks for them. Then they would reward us with a big fruit. Whether it was an orange or an apple, it was huge. I always wondered where they got those fruits from. I recently spoke to some new kids on the block. They told me that the new Jewish families don't ask them to come in anymore. I wonder why? Like the song goes, "these are ever changing times."

In this case though, I think change is for the worse. At least before when we did this service for the Jewish families, we were able to see how they lived. They told us why this was being done, and tried to explain their culture and religion to us. In return, we explained our culture and religion to them. Oh we still had our conflicts, but our conflicts we solved through neighborly mediations; not city politics.

Yea times have sure changed on "the block." New houses are going up all around it. Tony the tattoo guy is still on the next block; at the corner. He isn't going anywhere. The tattoo business is booming. When I was growing up only white guys tattooed. Now more Blacks are getting tattooed. It's the "in thing." Just look at all the basketball players who wear tattoos. Guys like Allen Iverson, Stephon Marbury, and Rasheed Wallace are filled with them.

The block is eerily quiet too! Nowadays, there's a soft silence resonating all over the block. And it appears more "hilly." Not as level as it once was. What the hell is going on! Am I getting older and more paranoid? Maybe. These things happen you know. The apartment buildings on "the block" have changed too. There is always a "for rent" sign on the facades of these buildings. Back in the day, you couldn't pry families out of those apartments. I remember one lady, Ms. Shirley... she was in her apartment for years. We hung out with her sons and daughters. She was very nice. When last I heard, she had moved too.

Albany Park is somewhat of a ghost town. Oh there are still kids playing ball there. But the Albany Park that we knew is no longer there; especially the movie watching and the picnics.   And there is no more camaraderie there. When we hung out there, we would play ball and hang out afterwards. We would sit around and drink some "drog," or "scheme" for some girl. Now people just play there and go home.

And the gangs?   This new bunch of guys have no ethics. They terrorize innocent people. The gangs in the past only did that when extremely necessary. They fought over turf, not what color bandana you had on your head. Besides, they all had gang jackets with the name of the gang emblazoned on the back. Just check out the movie "The Warriors." That's how it was back then. I mean hollywood distorted it a little bit, but you get the general idea.

Graffiti! That's another topic. Back in the day, we had great graffiti. Guys like "Lee," "Blade," and "Seen" were masters. They were legendary. "Futura 2000" was out of this world. Those guys should have been working on Madison Avenue. Nowadays the graffiti sucks. There is no detail, no 3-D, no colors, nothing. Just people writing over other people's names. Nothing artistic. The age of great graffiti is dead. Long live the good 'ole days of "Street Art."

Who knows! Maybe one day like a Phoenix, "the block" will rise again.

There was once a guy on the block who used to stutter worse than Claude. His name was Rennie. He used to especially stutter when he was lying, in trouble, or excited about something. Well maybe one day, we'll all take a page out of Rennie's book, and stutter with excitement; about a block resurgence.

Until then, we all have our memories. You can't take that away from us. Why would anyone want to!

The block is still in my veins. All who grew up there have what's known as "the block style." None of us are quitters. Never will be. We will also never kick another when he or she is down… that's "Brooklyn style".

"The block" is like a parody of tragedies and triumphs. We've had our share of both. It has never been boring on Lefferts Avenue and its surroundings; that's for sure. We wouldn't want it any other way.

Man, I didn't know an epilogue was so hard to finish. Part of me wants to put down the pen. Part of me wants to keep on writing. What the hell, I'll keep on writing. I owe myself and "the block" that much.

"The block." I wonder if there are, or were, other blocks like ours. I'm sure there were. There had to be. Why would fortune and misfortune, adventure and misadventure, and happiness and sadness only happen to one block; in one neighborhood and in one city. Then again, there was only one Martin Luther King; right?

About the Author

Brian O. was born forty years ago in Brooklyn, New York to Jamaican and Cuban parents. He was educated in the New York City Public School System. Mr. Smith graduated from Winthrop Junior High School and Erasmus Hall High School, where he was an art major.

Brian later went to college at City College of New York (C.C.N.Y.) where he majored in Health Administration. He received his Bachelor of Arts from City College in June 1982. Mr. Smith later went on to receive a Masters Degree in Public Health from Brooklyn College; in February 1990. He is an avid reader who loves sports, exercise and other recreational activities. Mr. Smith also enjoys drawing, painting, photography and computer graphics in his spare time.